D0970417

WORK FROM HOME AT ANY AGE

◆ ◆ ◆

J.J. Luna

Canary Islands Press
Arrecife de Lanzarote, Spain

Published by the Canary Islands Press
C/Benito Perez Armas, 12
35500 Arrecife de Lanzarote
Canary Islands, Spain

Case lots and special editions of this book are available at a discount. Please contact
R. Enriquez, U.S. Distributor
Canaryislands@hushmail.com

IBSN 0-9763872-3-9

Printed in Canada

FIRST EDITION

20 19 18 17 16 15 14 13 12 11 10 9 8 7 6 5 4 3 2 1

To Isabelita Coello, who quit school at age 14 and by persistence alone rose to become one of the finest wedding photographers in all Spain.

CONTENTS

◆ ◆ ◆

1
HELP IS ON THE WAY!

◆ ◆ ◆

When you have exhausted all possibilities, remember this—you haven't. – Thomas Edison

If you are older than 11, younger than 85, and are unhappy with your present circumstances, then this is the book you've been waiting for. As you will learn in the pages ahead, I made the biggest decision of my life before I turned 12. When I wrote my first book, I was already in my 70s, and I expect my most productive years to be ahead. If you find yourself described in one of the paragraphs below, this book will be especially helpful.

Still in high school

You are either undecided as to your future goals or you hope to go on to college, but you worry about the money problem.

Already in college

You have second thoughts about the career you've chosen, or you fear that good jobs will not be available in your field when you graduate.

Single parent with young children

Although forced to work away from home, you are desperate to spend more time with your kids in their formative years.

Parent of teenagers

You wonder if the kids *must* go on to college even though you and/or they will have to go tens of thousands of dollars into debt.

Unhappy employee

You are fed up with your job, your boss, your paycheck, and/or any prospects of security in the years to come.

Handicapped

You have disadvantages because of your race, religion, size, sex, illness, age or physical infirmity.

Bored with life

Nothing excites you anymore—not making new friends, not trying new foods, not even going on a trip. You feel shackled to an anchor that you cannot raise.

No star to guide you

You get no answers when you ask yourself questions such as "What am I here for?," "Why do bad things happen to good people?," and *"Is this all there is to life?"*

Baby boomer facing an uncertain future

You wish to change direction and try something new, but you're clueless as to what to do and how to do it.

Unhappy retiree

You have too much free time and not enough challenges, not enough adventure, not enough money.

Tired of living but afraid to die

Aha! You are the reader I am especially looking for! Keep reading, because help is on the way.

Author's qualifications

Has worked from home since 1960. I have started successful one-person home-based businesses again and again. The last one was just sold to a young man from Ohio for what has turned out to be an average price: $250,000. I'm now starting two more home-based businesses.

Beware of taking advice from anyone who's been in just one single business—that person may be like a one-trick pony. Case in point: A kid from my hometown was the original manager for the old musical group called Paul Revere and the Raiders. He lived like a millionaire in the late 1960s, spent it all, and has never been able to repeat his success.

Unafraid of change. In 1959, at the age of 31, I turned my year-old North Dakota barn-based business over to some friends, and—with my wife and small children in tow—caught a train to New York where we boarded the small Norwegian freighter *Ada Gorthon*. Nine days later, after weathering a violent storm in the North Atlantic, we came down the gangplank on Tenerife, one of Spain's Canary Islands off the coast of western Africa. Our lives were changed forever.

Choosing a star to steer by. I found what for me was a true purpose in life, and it has guided me ever since.

Understands the difference between a formal and a street-

The Lunas crossed the Atlantic on the Norwegian freighter *Ada Gorthon*, shown here upon arrival at Santa Cruz de Tenerife in November 1959.

smart education. I started with formal, but after spending three months alone in the summer of 1949, I cut my losses by not returning to the University of Minnesota to finish my senior year. My wife and I educated our children in three languages and then let them leave school before they were 16 to pursue other goals. For those of you who plan a career in teaching, law, or medicine, you must, of course, press on. But for the rest of you, I have some out-of-the-ordinary things to tell you.

And YOUR qualifications?

There is no quiz or test in this book as to whether or not you are suited to work for yourself because I do not consider any of the following to be a requirement.

- *Talent.* To quote our 30th president: "Nothing is more common than unsuccessful men with talent."
- *Handsome or beautiful.* These unfortunates get the false idea that their good looks will open doors that are closed to others. (Not even Tom Cruise or Julia Roberts can make it on looks alone.)
- *Raised with riches.* Too often it will be "rich kid, loser kid."
- *University education.* Tens of thousands of university graduates are currently working for a low wage in an unrelated field.
- *Above-average intelligence.* Intelligence alone will get you nowhere. (I used to have a good friend whose I.Q. was off the chart, and yet he ended up making some decisions so brainless that they defied all comprehension.)

There is, however, one quality that is absolutely essential for success in establishing your own business. As you read along, you will come to realize what that quality is. The good news is that even if you do not yet have this attribute, you can develop it at any age and regardless of your present circumstances!

Millionaire status

I was only a "thousandaire" when I retired from the North Dakota sign business, and making millions of dollars has never been a primary goal in my life. In fact, the first two times I had a chance to go that route (in 1969 and 1995), I walked away to pursue more important goals.

Some years ago, one of my business associates—Spain's famous modern artist Cesar Manrique—said to me after meeting a rather unpleasant client, "How sad it is to see someone whose only goal in life is making money!" (Cesar had built an exotic home in and under a vast lava field on Spain's Lanzarote Island for less than $120,000. Two years later, he received an offer of $1 million from a U.S. *Fortune 500* company whose directors were determined to buy it for a corporate retreat. He turned the offer down. "I already have a million dollars," he said, "and I intend to keep on living right where I am.")

I've started up a baker's dozen successful businesses on both sides of the Atlantic—all of them relatively small, simple, and interesting. "To love what you do," wrote Katherine Graham, owner of *The Washington Post*, "and feel that it matters—how could anything be more fun?" Here are a few of the topics that will be covered in the chapters ahead:

- How and why to work from home;
- How to find a niche and aim for the top of the market;
- Commonsense alternatives to a college education;
- How to keep your business small, simple, safe, and *private*;
- Astonishing benefits from time spent alone to read and meditate;
- How to dovetail your new business with the star you choose to steer by.

Can one simple book change anyone's life?

I've lost count of the number of readers of my previous book, *How to Be Invisible,* who wrote to say how it had positively changed their lives. Two readers insist that reading my book actually *saved* their lives because—since they had followed my suggestions—stalkers bent on murder were unable to track them down. More often, however, what the readers were saved from was worry, stress, and in a few cases, being served a subpoena for a frivolous lawsuit. As this present book was about to go to the printers, an e-mail came in from Craig Triance, a California lawyer. As best as I can remember, he wrote:

> I was already unhappy with the stress and long hours when I picked up your book [*How to Be Invisible*]. After reading it, I decided to close my downtown office, work from home, and limit myself to judgment collection only. I now look forward to every minute of my future simplified life!

Why I wrote this book

Day after day, I see men and women of all ages who are miserable in their jobs, drifting through life with no purpose, and who have no savings and no star to guide them. I meet young people who are planning to run up thousands of dollars in student debt to attend college merely because they think it's what they have to do. The resulting frustration has driven me to write *Work From Home at Any Age.* If my first book was helpful to many readers, I hope—and pray—that at least one of the things that I reveal in the pages ahead will produce a great change in *your* life.

What you will **not** *find in this book*

You will not find any list such as "101 best home-based businesses" because you must find your own unique angle or niche. Doubtless you've already seen some of those glowing advertisements in magazines or on the Internet that talk about mystery shopping, envelope stuffing, home typing, federal refund tracing, jobs involving photography and scanning, and so forth.

The promises in those advertisements are almost invariably lies.

Nor will I recommend franchises. Franchises cost money, often tens or even hundreds of thousands of dollars, whereas my advice is to start out from scratch. Invest your *time* rather than any serious amount of money.

This is the information that **does** *await you*

You will learn how to find or create your own niche, how to make a good first impression, how to keep your business invisible to others, and why a street-smart education may give you or your children a head start over university graduates. You will also find out how to seek and use solitude, and you will learn a method for finding a true purpose in life that you otherwise might never consider.

In the next chapter, you'll discover how to put money in your pocket *fast*, along with information about what money can and cannot do. You'll learn how children differ between wealthy and middle-class families, why renting is usually better than owning, and the only way to ever buy a vehicle. The chapter will close by exposing two dangerous myths about money.

You may not agree with everything I have to say. A few of my suggestions, in fact, may raise your blood pressure. Should that occur, just stay calm, take a deep breath, and skip ahead to the chapter that follows. Okay? Then let's get started. Fasten your seatbelt. And enjoy the ride!

2
A COMMONSENSE VIEW OF MONEY

◆ ◆ ◆

Give me neither poverty nor riches.

– Agur, Proverbs 30:8

Although money can't buy happiness, the lack of money can absolutely guarantee *un*happiness, so let's discuss a remedy.

When I was in my early 20s, I continuously traveled around the state of Montana, selling health and accident insurance to farmers living in the remotest parts of the state. Even though my earnings were slim, I always did my best to carry a portrait of Grover Cleveland in the form of a $1,000 bill. (Yes, Virginia, $1,000 bills really did circulate freely in those days.) This was my rainy-day fund, never to be touched except in an emergency such as sickness or a blown engine on my '46 Packard. When I did have to break a bill at the bank, I then worked all the harder and spent almost nothing on myself until I could earn at least a $500 (William McKinley) bill, and as soon thereafter as possible, I was back to carrying Grover Cleveland's portrait.

In 1950, $1,000 was equivalent to what $10,000 will buy today, but since the largest bill in circulation since 1969 is the $100 bill, it would take a hundred such bills to make $10,000—rather bulky to stuff into your pocket or purse. Furthermore, if the police should ever catch you with $10,000 in cash, they'd figure you were dealing drugs and would confiscate your money. One thousand, however, is a reasonable goal, and if you cannot yet put that much together, I urge you not to rest until you get it.

Before the sun rises tomorrow morning, make a vow not to spend anything for nonessentials until you get that backup money put together. No eating out, no buying sodas or beer, no movies, no cable TV, no unnecessary trips around town, no newspapers or magazines, no lattes, no presents for anyone no matter what the occasion, no tithing, no nothing—*nada en absoluto.* If you're renting an upscale home, drop down to a small apartment. If you're already in a small apartment, perhaps you could rent a single room somewhere, or even go back home. Do not tell me it cannot be done. I know Mexicans working two or three jobs at minimum wage who send hundreds of dollars to their wives or parents in Mexico *every month.*

Still think you can't cut it? Just imagine that, no matter how secure your present job is, you're going to lose it six months from today, with no final paycheck and no unemployment compensation. Assume that once you lose the job, it may be six months before you find another one. If you really believed that in your heart and soul, would you not stop all nonessential spending? So, believe it, because lightning can strike from a clear blue sky, and your paychecks could disappear when you least expect it.

Note: $1,000 feels a lot better in your pocket than it does in a bank, and $1,000, in any event, is just a stopgap measure. Your true goal should be a bedrock minimum of the value of a 1950 $1,000 bill, i.e., $10,000: $1,000 in cash (divided between your pocket and a secure hiding place at home) and $9,000 more in the bank.

The problem with too much

Many of you are familiar with the pain that comes from running completely out of cash. Incredible as it may seem, the pain at the opposite end can be equally intense.

Consider *The New York Times* obituary of October 29, 1993, with the headline: "DORIS DUKE, 80, HEIRESS WHOSE GREAT WEALTH COULDN'T BUY HAPPINESS, IS DEAD." The article said that late one evening in Rome in 1945, Miss Duke, who was then 33 years old, told a friend that her vast fortune was in some ways a barrier to happiness. "All that money is a problem sometimes," she said. "After I've gone out with a man a few times, he starts to tell me how much he loves me. But how can I know if he really means it? How can I ever be sure?" The *Times* noted: "Her words that night showed that her life had been profoundly affected, even scarred, by her wealth."

Listen to John Paul Getty, once reputed to be the richest man in the world. Two years before his death, a reporter asked him if money had brought him happiness.

"Money," he answered, "doesn't necessarily have any connection with happiness. Maybe with unhappiness."

Actress Jane Fonda, Ted Turner's ex, was once quoted as saying, "I've had my taste of wealth and all the material things. They don't mean a thing. There's a psychiatrist that goes with every swimming pool out here, not to mention divorces and children who hate their parents."

"The show and splendor of great houses, elaborate furnishings, stately halls, oppress me; impose upon me," wrote American essayist and naturalist John Burroughs a century ago. "They fix the attention on false values, they set up a false standard of beauty; they stand between me and the real feeders of character and thought."

Can money bring happiness to your children?

Think about this question seriously. Will your children love you more because you spent time away from them to get rich, or will they love you more because you were always there for them?

According to a report from the Alfred P. Sloan Foundation, when it comes to children, there is an inverse relationship between money and happiness. A survey was made between two groups: those from middle-class families and those from wealthy families. The children from the middle class said they were happier. (Although the report didn't specify the reasons why rich kids were less happy, I can guess that it was from being raised by nannies, fed by cooks, driven by chauffeurs, and in some cases ending up in homes broken by separations or divorces.)

A few, however, have avoided the dangers that come with wealth. One such person is movie director Chris Columbus (*Home Alone, Harry Potter*) who, when he was starting out in New York City, lived in a place with mice and rats. He has this to say about the pros and cons of wealth when it comes to the children:

> You can certainly have nice dinners. And you don't have to live in a place with mice and rats. . . . But the only thing money provides is a level of security. We never had nannies for our kids or cooks or any of those things. It takes away from families' lives. . . . I learned it by seeing other families in the film business sort of destroy their families by having too many other people around. The kids didn't know who their parents were.
>
> – *The Detroit News,* January 3, 2005

To the above I would add one additional observation: Since children compare themselves to their peers, they will often be more content if they have *slightly* more than their friends as opposed to slightly less. This explains why my sister and I were perfectly content growing up in a tiny house with no utilities whatsoever. We had all the firewood we needed to keep warm during the bitter winters, and we had good meals year-round, whereas some of our classmates went both cold and hungry.

The same principle applied when my wife and I raised our children in the Canary Islands. For the first few years we lived simply, with few of the luxuries so common to children in North America. Nevertheless, our scale of living was above that of our neighbors. Our children, therefore, felt that we as a family were a bit more fortunate than our neighbors were, despite the fact that the neighbors had TV sets whereas I wouldn't allow one in our home.

Money from heaven?

Do you buy lottery tickets? If so, over your lifetime, you may lose tens of thousands of your hard-earned dollars. A more serious problem, however, is the remote possibility of winning the jackpot. More tears are shed from winning a lottery than from losing one. Here is one of a long litany of complaints about striking it rich, taken from an Associated Press dispatch on December 14, 2004:

> The wife of the lottery winner who took home the richest undivided jackpot in U.S. history says she regrets his purchase of the $314.9 million ticket that has thrust her family into the public spotlight.
>
> "I wish all of this never would have happened," Jewel Whittaker told *The Charleston Gazette* for Tuesday's editions. "I wish I would have torn the ticket up."

> Since winning the lottery two years ago, her husband, Jack Whittaker, has been arrested twice for drunken driving and has been ordered into rehab. He pleaded no contest Monday to a misdemeanor assault charge for attacking a bar manager, and is accused in two lawsuits of making trouble at a nightclub and a racetrack . . . "

Remember, I am not talking about wealth slowly accumulated through your own efforts, a course that—if handled in moderation—can bring you deep satisfaction. I'm talking about getting a huge sum of money *without having worked for it*, whether from a jackpot, a lottery, or even from an inheritance. The frequent result is that an unexpected windfall may not be "money from heaven."

More likely, it'll be money from hell.

The road to freedom

A ship has no freedom until the anchor is raised. The way to raise the anchor on your ship is to eliminate mortgage payments, car payments, and payments for any other loans.

To eliminate mortgage payments, rent rather than own your home. Many of you may consider this advice to be shocking. Nevertheless, I stand by it, especially for those of you who are just starting out and think you need a "starter" home. For one thing, renting is normally cheaper.

However, this is not the main reason for renting rather

than owning. If you rent from month to month, you are free to pack up on short notice and move, whereas I've seen homes stay on the market for a year or even two before being sold or repossessed. Here are a few of the many reasons why you may suddenly wish to leave an area earlier than you now expect:

- One of the neighbors is unbelievably obnoxious.
- Another neighbor has a dog that barks all night.
- A drug dealer or a child molester moves into your area.
- Your in-laws start shopping for a house on your street.
- A stalker has targeted you, and the police cannot protect you 24/7.
- A job or business opportunity opens up in a faraway state.
- A friend in Hawaii invites you to come on over and says he'll help you get settled.
- You get laid off or fired, and the job market in your area is in the pits.
- Your 16-year-old daughter sneaks out at night to see her 25-year-old tattooed, earring-laden boyfriend who's an industrial-strength loser. You need to move to the Aleutian Islands—fast. (If you can cope with 16-hour shifts, there are high-paying jobs there on the crab-fishing boats working the Bering Sea out of Dutch Harbor.)
- Although innocent, you are about to be arrested for a horrific crime, and you have no alibi that will stand up in court. You need to pack up *tonight* and race to Canada, Mexico, or the Turks and Caicos Islands.

Do my wife and I practice what we teach? Absolutely. We rented until we returned from the Canary Islands some years ago to care for my wife's mother. Since we knew this would tie us down for a few years, and because we had more than enough cash to make the purchase, we bought our first home (1,400 square feet) on the outskirts of Carson City, Nevada. Since then, we've moved a few times and in each case bought homes for cash. However, in every instance, we were—and are—free to move. We can just leave the home behind for eventual resale because there is no mortgage to hold us back. In fact, in a worst-case scenario, we can *lose* the home without altering our lifestyle because we'll just rent a comparable place elsewhere. One great thing about money—unlike time—is that if you lose it, you can replace it.

If you are presently buying a home, and do not yet have at least $10,000 set aside in an emergency fund, consider this: Sell your home, set aside $10,000 from the equity, use the balance—if any—to live on while you start a new business.

Buy used vehicles only, and pay cash. In North America, used cars are so cheap that almost anyone can avoid car payments by making a cash purchase. Japanese cars may cost more than American or European makes, but as long as the mileage is under 150,000, they should keep you going for several years without any major repairs.

Although I've sometimes bought a car, driven it for six months or a year, and sold it for the same as I paid, I lay no claim to being the all-time winner for cheap transportation. That credit goes to Maria G., a petite señorita from southern

Utah. I asked her to send me an e-mail with the story of her current car, and here's what she wrote:

> Well, Jack, I didn't check the oil of my old car, so I killed my cute little red Honda Civic. From previous experience, however, I knew that you can get a really good deal on transportation if you buy a car that's been in an accident but has an excellent engine. I watched the classifieds and found an ad for a vehicle that had body damage, so the owners were only asking $300. My dad and I went to see it, and sure enough, the owner had just finished paying for it when a woman ran straight into the passenger side of the vehicle, and so the door was smashed in so badly you couldn't even open the door. When I test drove it, the engine ran great. Only 101,000 miles on the 1988 323 Mazda! So my dad said it was a good deal, and we bought it. When we got home, my dad took the door completely off its hinges and pounded it until he was able to put the door back on and at least be able to open and close it when needed. As of this March [2005], I've driven it over 65,000 miles, and it's never needed any major repairs except the usual maintenance for any vehicle. I figure it will go at least 35,000 more miles, and after that, I'll sell it and get at least $200 of my $300 back.

Do the math: $100 depreciation divided by 100,000 miles represents a cost of $.001 per mile, or 10 miles for a penny.

Contrast that with the original owner, who Maria says had "just finished paying for it" when the accident occurred. The interest alone must have been substantial.

If you are low on cash right now and need transportation, perhaps you can do as Maria did. Granted, it may take a lot of time to find such a car, but if you do, don't take the car to a body shop to have it fixed. Hammer out enough sheet metal so the doors will open and the wheels will go around, and then drive it as is. Wear those dents like a badge of honor, and laugh all the way to the bank.

A good second choice is to buy a 7- to 10-year-old Japanese-made car from a private party, preferably from the original owner. "One owner" usually means the car has been faithfully serviced and tenderly cared for. It may serve you well for a year or two, after which time you may choose to move up. When you do, however, buy again from a private party.

When a new car is needed. This may be for a special occasion, a business trip, or for a two-week vacation with the kids. Just head down to Enterprise Rent-A-Car, and choose something nice. (Despite negative reviews, we still like Kia Amantis and rent them whenever they are available.) You don't even need a credit card because Enterprise will accept a cash deposit in lieu of a credit card.

"Going broke on $33 million a year"

That was the headline on the front page of *Newsweek* on February 24, 1997. Listed alongside the headline were Loni

Anderson, Dorothy Hamill, Shannen Dougherty, Burt Reynolds, Kim Basinger and M. C. Hammer (who went from $33 million a year to zero). Inside were the pictures of more losers, including Wayne Newton, Susan Powter, Bjorn Borg, and Willie Nelson.

Does this tell you something? The reason that the "millionaires next door" have a million is because they consistently spend less than they earn, and they seldom pay retail. Many, in fact, go to yard sales and shop the thrift stores, as do we. Start today to spend less than you earn.

Two myths about money

Myth #1: Money is very important in life.

Money is only important until you have enough to cover your needs. From that point on, it is less and less important. Beyond a certain point, in fact, there is a law of diminishing returns. This explains not only why so many rich people are miserable but why their spouses are miserable (e.g., divorces) and why their children are so miserable (e.g., drugs and alcohol).

Myth #2: Money is very difficult to obtain.

If you live in a third-world country such as Chad, Sudan, or the Cape Verde Islands, then yes, it is indeed difficult to obtain. But if you live in the United States, Canada, Australia, or Europe, then you can earn money even without a job and with little if any capital. All it takes is a decent idea and a little nerve—as is outlined in the chapter to follow.

IMMEDIATE STEPS

- Do whatever it takes to set aside an emergency fund, even just $1,000.
- Eliminate all monthly payments on debt. Pay cash, or do without.
- As long as you live, never *ever* seek money itself as a worthwhile goal in life.

Suggested Reading

The Total Money Makeover, by Dave Ramsey (Nelson Books, 2003.) Ramsey urges you to work hard, put together a thousand-dollar emergency fund as soon as possible, pay what you owe, and then stay out of debt from that point on.

3
START OUT WITH A VERY SMALL BANG

◆ ◆ ◆

Small opportunities are often the beginning of great enterprises. – *Demosthenes*

You may remember reading about the European sailing ship that was becalmed for weeks off the coast of Brazil, causing its occupants to run out of fresh water. When they signaled a small Portuguese fishing boat and pantomimed that they were dying of thirst, one of the fishermen lowered a bucket into the sea, pulled it up, drank from it, and then motioned that they should do the same. *The water was fresh.* The sailing ship was off the mouth of the Amazon—a river that discharges fresh water more than 100 miles into the Atlantic.

The parallel is that if you find yourself stranded in a depressed area where no jobs are available, it may be that money—although not visible to others—is nevertheless available if you know how and where to look.

Before I left home on the morning after graduating from

high school, my father gave me two rules for making my way in the world. The first and most important one was "If you want to make money, go to where the money is circulating." The second one was "Never take a partner."

I'd already seen a classic example of rule number one from my mother's brother. That was when I was in grade school—the Depression years of the 1930s. Frank and Judy Peterson owned their own small country home in a severely depressed area along the northern border of Minnesota. Frank had a home woodworking shop and a talent for making small items out of scraps of wood. There were no jobs available for this limited talent, but Frank wasn't looking for a job, he was looking for an income.

During the long, dark winter months, with temperatures dropping to -40° and -50°, Frank turned out wooden trains, custom mailboxes, house numbers, knife holders, silhouette wall hangings, jewelry boxes, birdhouses, puzzles for kids, and lawn ornaments of all kinds. His wife painted them as fast as he could produce them, using up five-gallon buckets of enamel paint purchased directly from a wholesaler.

When spring came and the snow thawed, the Petersons packed a covered utility trailer with their products, hooked it up to a Ford V-8, and headed for the rich farming area near the Iowa border 400 miles to the south. The Depression had not much affected the well-to-do farmers in this area, and so the unique wooden items were quickly sold. From May through September, they made one trip south each month. On the return trip, they loaded their trailer with scrap wood purchased for a song from carpenter and cabinet shops along the way. These five trips netted enough profit to live well all year round at a time when over 30 percent of their county's residents were unemployed.

In many cases today, of course, you need not physically go to where the money is circulating. With the advent of overnight courier services and the Internet, you can reach out across the country or around the world and bring the money back to wherever you live, depressed though the area may be. In fact, a depressed area may be the *best* place to live, given the lower cost of rentals and real estate.

You need never be unemployed if you work for yourself

It doesn't matter what your sex or age is or where you live or who you know or whether you just lost your job and your savings are fast disappearing. The tips and suggestions in the pages to follow are not based on any pie-in-the-sky theories. Rather, they are based upon my own personal experiences over a long lifetime. Although there were some ups and downs in the early years, I learned from my mistakes. By the time I was 30, I was off and running. Some of my successful home-based businesses have been:

- Outdoor signs;
- Short story writer;
- Commercial photo murals;
- High-society wedding albums;
- Unique burglar alarm systems;
- Land development projects overseas;

- Incorporating Europeans in Wyoming;
- Selling privacy reports via mail order;
- Stock signs for bars, cafés, and auto sales;
- Advertising specialties for a niche market;
- Magnetic signs (when they first came out);
- Self-published travel booklets for tourist areas;
- Fine art figure studies for camera magazines and photography annuals;
- A Canadian banking report, plus mail-drop information sold via the Internet.

"A man at work"

The blind professor at the University of Minnesota perched on the corner of his desk, removed his opaque glasses, and opened our freshman class in economics with these words: "There are only two ways to produce income: a *man* at work or a *dollar* at work."

That was at a time when it was universally understood that "man" referred to men or women equally. In this book, to avoid the ungainly "he/she" and "him/her," I use the word "man" in the sense that the professor did. Just keep in mind that this book is written for *you,* whether you are a teenage boy, a single mother, a man in a midlife crisis, or an elderly lady.

In my highly subjective opinion, a new business should be started with "a man at work." Few, if any, dollars should be added, either at the beginning or later. Let your new business be debt-free from the very beginning, and then pay its own way!

How one business was started for less than a dollar

> *"Out of hope, out of rope, out of time."*
> – William Cobbs, *The Hudsucker Proxy*

Before I entered the University of Minnesota in the fall of 1946, I rented a basement bedroom from an elderly widow, a Mrs. Dora Johnson. Her rambling old house, which included a large yard with giant oaks, sat in the shadow of the football stadium in St. Paul. The rent was due, and I'd exhausted my supply of the four basic food groups: bread, peanut butter, milk, and Kraft Dinner. Nevertheless, although low on both time and rope, hope remained.

The following day, there'd be a big game at the stadium—the Minnesota Gophers were on a roll that fall—and the stadium's few parking lots would fill long before the game began. Gopher fans would then be on the prowl for parking spaces along residential streets for half a mile around.

"Mrs. Johnson," I said, "before the game tomorrow, can I take down a section of your fence and park cars on your lawn?"

"Goodness gracious, I don't want you taking down any of my fence, and the cars would hurt the grass."

"The grass won't be hurt much in a single day, ma'am, and of course I'd put the fence back just like it was. I'd charge a dollar a car and split the money with you fifty-fifty."

"*A dollar a car?* Well . . . how many cars could we park here?"

"Twenty, perhaps more. Every time there's a game, it would be like free money coming in."

"Land sakes a'goshen!"

I bought a half-pint can of paint for 49 cents, borrowed an old brush from my landlady, and had a section of the fence down before sunrise the next morning. A three-foot-square, hand-painted cardboard sign was nailed to a tree on the far side of the opening, with eight-inch letters painted in fire-engine red:

PARK HERE

➡ ➡ ➡

$1.00

"Leave your keys in the ignition," I said as each car pulled in. "I'll park it myself and guard it until you come back." (Note to Minnesota historians: this marked the first-ever valet parking for the St. Paul stadium.) I fitted the cars in among the oaks as if they were pieces of a jigsaw puzzle. Some were jammed in so tightly that I had to exit through a passenger-side window. Once the yard was filled right out to the sidewalk, I tallied the take on the widow's kitchen table.

"Twenty-six $1 bills, Mrs. Johnson, and $3 in change. Twenty-nine bucks. Your share," I said, counting it out, "is $14.50."

"Why, you *darling* boy!"

We continued our joint venture for the rest of the season, splitting the proceeds each time. Although you younger readers may not be impressed, you should know that in the years following World War II, a nickel could buy you a ride across Minneapolis on the streetcar or a juicy hamburger at the White

Castle on Washington Avenue S.E. My room rent was just $3 a week.

Charge 50 percent in advance

In 1958, I started an illuminated Plexiglas sign business in the little one-saloon town of Powers Lake, North Dakota, which, at that time, was 40 miles from the nearest paved road. Although our little rental house had no garage, my friend Eiler Anderson had some available space. He'd just moved his custom combining equipment out of an old barn and into a new steel building, so he offered me the use of the barn at no charge.

The next problem was cash. I was down to less than $100, and I needed at least $600 to buy materials: a small jigsaw and a second-hand "brake" that would be needed to bend sheet metal. I had an idea, and I drove to Minot, North Dakota, to test it out.

First, I bought a pad of generic order blanks at Olson's Office Supply. Next, I drove around Minot in search of a building that needed a sign. Thirty minutes later, I stopped in front of a building that was just being completed, and introduced myself to the owner. This was to be the new home of Braasch Plumbing Supplies, and yes, he was shopping for a sign. I offered to sketch a few ideas. (One of my few talents is a flair for drawing in three dimensions.) At the end of nearly two hours, with wrinkled sheets of paper all over the floor, I came up with a design that Mr. Braasch liked.

"How much?"

"That's a $6,000 sign at any sign shop, but I'm just starting out, and I want your business. Four thousand total. Half in advance."

His $2,000 check set me up in business.

No borrowed money, no big bang

Although I have no guaranteed recipe for success, I have a dandy one for failure: Make a BIG BANG using borrowed money. So, go for the small bang, and the smaller the better.

What you need is not borrowed money; you need to find or create a unique angle or niche. And you will learn all about that in the following chapter.

REVIEW

- *Go to where money is circulating*, or bring the money home to you.
- *Start out small.* Never rent an office away from home. (If you need more space, rent a larger home with a big upstairs, a daylight basement, and/or a three-car garage.)
- *Keep everything simple*. Do not take a partner, hire an employee, or open a retail business. Do not buy a franchise. Start from scratch.

Suggested reading

Unstoppable: 45 Powerful Stories of Perseverance and Triumph from People Just Like You by Cynthia Kersey (Sourcebooks Trade, 1998.)

This is an unusually inspirational book with real stories of real people. Read about Bill Porter, who developed cerebral palsy as a result of a difficult birth. As he grew up, it was assumed he was mentally deficient, and yet he rose to become the top salesman in the Watkins Company's entire western division and has been featured on both *20/20* and CNN! You'll also read about the young boy who walked barefoot across Africa in search of his dream. His is an unbelievable story!

4
HOW TO FIND OR CREATE YOUR OWN NICHE

◆ ◆ ◆

I don't want to be left behind. In fact, I want to be here before the action starts. – *Kerry Packer (Australia's richest man and media magnate)*

On the East Coast, niche rhymes with quiche, whereas in the West, niche rhymes with rich. However you pronounce it, you may not get rich with a niche but you'll certainly fail fast if you don't find one. Since 1960, all of my businesses have been in niche markets with little or no competition.

Definition of a niche

My Compact Oxford English Dictionary says one of the definitions of a niche is "a specialized but profitable corner of the market." This market niche can be a geographic area, a specialty industry, an ethnic or age group, or any other particular group of people. Sometimes a niche product can be a variation of a common product that is not produced and marketed by the main marketing firms.

The following examples are from three of my own businesses.

Alarmas Electronicas

Until 1969, there was virtually no crime in the Canary Islands. However, that changed the following year when foreign sailors began to wait until their freighter or tanker was about to depart. They would then smash the window of a jewelry store, grab what they could, race back to their ship, and be back on the high seas before the crime could be reported.

Since I'd just sold my photo mural business and was looking for something new, news items about these recent burglaries caught my eye. I checked around. No one in the area—so far—was in the burglar alarm business, so I found and then ordered a $55 instruction manual from the United States. The moment it arrived, I studied it, underlining important parts of it. Then I ordered the necessary relays, bells, tapes, control boxes, and magnetic switches from Ademco Inc. in Long Island, New York, and started selling alarm systems to jewelry stores on the two main islands: Tenerife and Gran Canaria.

Although my first alarm systems were simple, it was said that my prices were unusually high (true), but where else could the jewelers go? A costly alarm system was far better than no alarm system at all! Later, when competition began to appear on the horizon, I quickly sold the little business to a British friend. He later sold out to a German group, and the business grew to become what is now called Grupo 4—one of Spain's largest alarm system companies. (Note: When we later moved to the small outer island of Lanzarote, I planned to start a new alarm business there. However, it turned out that there were as yet no burglars on this island, so I had to either import burglars or find some other niche.)

Lesson learned: This was only a niche because no one else was doing it yet. When competition appeared, I quickly sold out. If you live in a small city, you can do something similar by being the first one to bring in a type of business that is already doing well in larger cities. Or, if you live in a large city, scout out smaller cities and move to one that does not yet have whatever business you are interested in starting.

Jennifer Basye Sander, in her book *Niche and Grow Rich*, tells the story of a 23-year-old girl in Sacramento, California, who was sick of working in politics and decided to do something else. She recalled that when she was in college, she'd purchased a little directory of women-owned businesses in the San Francisco Bay area. Since no similar directory was available in Sacramento, she produced *The Sacramento Women's Yellow Pages,* and it turned out to be a sales sensation.

Nevada corporations

When we returned to the United States in 1988, we settled down in Nevada, the home state for literally hundreds of incorporators who were then advertising in *USA Today*, *The Wall Street Journal*, and numerous entrepreneurial magazines.

I didn't know much about Nevada corporations, but I'd had both a corporation and a limited liability company (LLC) in the Canary Islands, so that was a start. I bought some books, took a lawyer to lunch, and finally spotted a niche. Not a single incorporator was going after sales in Europe.

I ran a one-inch display ad in the Paris-based *International Herald Tribune.* The headline was **NEVADA CORPORATIONS**, and it was aimed directly at the PT crowd. ("PT" can refer to anything from "Private Travelers" to "Permanent Tourists" and refers to the approximately 500,000 Europeans who live for a few months in one country, then a few months in another, and never settle down long enough to get on any tax rolls. They use a variety of corporations to hold real estate and bank accounts anonymously.)

My ad listed only a fax number. I answered incoming faxes each day beginning at 2 A.M., which was 10 A.M. in the UK and 11 A.M. in continental Europe. It took me a year to build up a reputation for reliability and lightning-fast service, during which time I discovered that Wyoming corporations were better for privacy than Nevada. At the end of that year, once it was decided that I was their man in America, the word traveled fast among the PT folks. When the incorporation business took off like a homesick angel, I withdrew my ad from the Paris newspaper and never had to advertise again. By 1974, it was taking up too much of my time, so I sold it to a Bellevue, Washington, entrepreneur for $500,000 and retired for a year. The Bellevue buyer—who works alone in his home office and never runs an ad—is now a millionaire.

Lesson learned: This is an example of selling a common product to uncommon buyers—in this case the well-to-do European PT crowd.

I took a similar approach on the little island of Lanzarote. Tourism was just coming to the island, and the hotels, villas, and condos were being built only along the southern beaches. The constant sun made up for the desert-like landscape, the Coney Island atmosphere, and the lack of a view. Prices for land in this area went into the stratosphere. Therefore, I bought up cheap land along the high northern cliffs where it was often rainy (and therefore green) and where the only neighbors would be a few scattered farmers. The niche buyers were a small number of expatriates from northern Europe who—for year-round living—preferred a greener landscape, a lower cost, an isolated location, and the view from an 800-meter cliff.

The "Personal Privacy Report"

I've valued my privacy ever since my early years in Spain, so it was natural to keep an eye out for any books on that subject. However, although many books had been published about privacy, not one of them had practical and legal solutions to everyday problems. Might there be a niche here? I decided to test the waters.

Between 1997 and 1998, I put together a "Personal Privacy Report." I printed several of them out on my laser printer and assembled each one in a three-ring binder. To sell my reports, I purchased a mailing list of well-to-do people who had shown interest in protecting themselves by purchasing a book called *How to Outfox the Foxes* by Larry Williams (CTI Pub., 1991). The first mailing was a test; I sent out 200 signed letters first class, offering a free brochure called "Ten Tips for Personal Privacy." Nine requests came back, so I started mailing out hundreds of letters offering the free booklet, then thousands.

Each person who answered received the free brochure plus a personal letter and a gilt-edged order blank for the "Personal Privacy Report." It sold well at $99, so I upped the price to $197, then $297, then $397, and finally $497. Sales were steady up to $297 but dropped sharply at $397 and disappeared at $497. OK, so $297 would be the fixed price with an offer for money back if not satisfied for the first two years. (The return rate was only 2 percent.)

By the time I'd run through all the names on the *How to Outfox the Foxes* list, I'd sold 377 reports, but this was getting to be hard work. Why not just sell it as a book? Finding an agent turned out to be far more difficult than writing the report, but after 10 months and 41 strikeouts, I snagged a New York literary agent. He promptly sold the book to St. Martin's Press.

Lesson learned: There is no better way to become an expert in any given field than to research and write a definitive book.

When *How to Be Invisible* first hit the bookstores, coupled with an article by me in *Playboy* and an interview on the *G. Gordon Liddy Show*, the book rose to number 37 in

Amazon's top bestsellers list for August 2000. It has remained their best-selling book in the field of personal privacy and is now available in a completely revised version. The royalties from the book, however, are inconsequential compared to the fact that I am now considered to be *the* authority on privacy and can charge hundreds of dollars an hour plus time and expenses as a consultant for personal privacy and security. You can imitate this success even if you are not a writer. Hire a ghost writer, and then publish the book yourself.

Avoid this common error

"Find a need, and serve it." (Quoted from ISU/Belmont University Business classes, among others.)

Bad advice!

You can go broke trying to serve a need. What you must do is create a *want,* and serve it. No one on the planet *needs* a Rolls Royce, a diamond ring, or a Rolex, but many people buy them.

> At one party, a woman was seen wearing a Rolex watch on her left wrist and a cheap Timex with large numbers on the other wrist. When asked about this strange combination, she said, "The Rolex is for you. The Timex is for me."

An example of finding then checking out a niche

In the late summer of 1993, during a hot spell in Reno, Nevada, I bought an Acura Legend from a private party. I quickly discovered that unless the car had been parked in the shade, the air conditioner could not cool the car down. I took it to a local dealer who told me it was a design flaw that had no remedy!

Although I didn't *need* to be cool, I certainly *wanted* to be cool, and I was positive that other Acura Legend owners wanted to be cool as well. So then, if this problem could be solved, a new business could be started. At the time, I was already busy enough with another enterprise, but I had a friend (I'll refer to him as "Casper") who was looking for work. If I could set something up, Casper might be the ideal man to take something like this and run with it, but first I had to answer this question: *How could a car always stay in the shade?* I thought back to our early days in the Canary Islands.

Land Rovers in Spain. Before SUVs ever came on the scene, Land Rovers were being built for General Franco's Guardia Civil (Civil Guards). Summer temperatures rose to 105° in southern Spain and even higher in the desert, and these vehicles had no air conditioning. What they did have, however, was a double roof. Land Rovers at that time were even boxier than they are today, and the roofs were flat. A second roof was mounted over the first, with about an inch of space in between. Except for narrow supports, the sides and ends were open so that air passed freely under the second roof. The lower roof was therefore always in the shade.

Car-top carrier for photo murals. When I was making photo murals for offices, bars, and resort hotels in the late

1960s, I needed a way to deliver the mounted pictures, which were up to 5 feet wide and 12 feet long. The solution was to build a metal rack that held a plywood platform over the entire car, which was held up by pipes attached to the front and rear bumpers.

One of the author's thousands of photo murals that decorate hotel rooms, professional offices, restaurants, and private homes in the Canary Islands. The picture shown here is El Teide (12,292 ft.) on the island of Tenerife.

One summer, we decided to drive to the Spanish mainland, so we took this car—a big Opel Commodore—with the overhead rack and boarded a ferry that took us to Cadiz. We drove off the ferry early one morning and headed north to see the ancient Roman ruins in Mérida. Cars in those days did not normally come with air conditioning, but we were doing fine until we stopped for gas at about 11 A.M. When I opened the door, it was like opening it next to a blast furnace! All that saved us on that trip through southern Spain was the rooftop platform. We were always in the shade.

The solution to my current Acura Legend problem was obvious: Build and sell a car-top shade.

Go to the top. Since, according to Frank Lloyd Wright, "form and function should be one," I would need to have someone design a car-top shade contoured so that even at high speeds, it would not lift off, vibrate, or whistle. Who better to talk to about air flow than Burt Rutan, the famous founder of Scaled Composites? (He's even more famous today after designing and building Space Ship One, the aircraft that claimed the $10 million Ansari X Prize.) At 3:00 the next morning, I took off from Carson City and headed south on U.S. 395.

Six and a half hours later, I entered the air-conditioned offices of Scaled Composites in Mojave, California, and told the receptionist that I'd just arrived from Carson City, Nevada, to see Mr. Burt Rutan. I was told that Burt was away on a trip but was asked if I would like to speak to the general manager. Of course. The GM listened to my idea carefully, took it seriously, discussed it as an expert, and took me in to see some of the composites they worked with, as well as several exotic aircraft under construction.

I left Scaled Composites with an estimate of $18,000 to produce a basic design. Once I placed the order and made a deposit, they would experiment with a variety of shapes, testing them on one of their cars that would race back and forth down the airstrip at 100 miles an hour.

On the long drive back to Carson City, I had time to think. At least I didn't have to worry about finding a niche. This was a new field, wide open.

Keep it simple. What if Acura owners turned up their noses at the design? Also, what about all the other cars on the road? If each model required a different shade, this whole idea was going to become too complicated. I decided to change the plan and aim at the tens of thousands of old cars with either no air conditioning or air conditioning that didn't work and was too expensive to repair. A lot of Mexicans who work in the fields in the Southwest might go for something like this, but the shades would have to be inexpensive.

Hmmm . . .what about using old newspapers wetted down with glue and pressed into a mold? Strengthen them with chicken wire inside, spray on some waterproof paint, and they should last for one season. I'd have repeat business that way, and if one of the shades did break up sometime, flying newspaper would be a lot safer than flying metal.

What about appearance? With a smooth surface, the tops could be sprayed with a reflective aluminum coating, and the bottoms painted in a neutral gray. Maybe some small turned-up fins along the sides to jazz it up.

Keep it down to three sizes, at least to start. Small for Japanese cars, large for the big American models, and one for full-sized pickups. Test them only at lower speeds, and warn the buyers there might be some wind noise on the highway.

Never invest without a test. At no point did I consider hiring employees, renting a building, and producing the car shades en masse. Rather, once a mock-up was made and shown around in Southern California, most of my work would be over. I could help out with a few hundred dollars to make the mock-up, and Casper could take it from there. If the interest warranted it, I might later lend Casper the money to have Scaled Composites prepare the three basic forms, perhaps to be molded in fiberglass. I couldn't wait to tell him about this terrific new opportunity.

Not everything works out. Casper failed to share my enthusiasm for car-top shades. Without enthusiasm, failure would be certain. I talked to another person about it who responded in the same way, so the idea went on the shelf. I still think the idea is sound, so if any of you want to take it and run with it, be my guest.

As for my round trip south to Mojave, there were no regrets. The long drive had been worth it just for the fascinating tour through Scaled Composites.

What to do next if your new venture fails

Had I not had another business to run at the time, I would have had a low-cost mock-up built to cover the roof of my Acura, whether it whistled and vibrated or not. Then I'd have taken it down to El Centro—just north of Mexicali—and parked it in some central location with big signs in English and Spanish, perhaps something like this:

ASK ME ABOUT THIS CAR-TOP SHADE
THAT WILL HELP KEEP YOU COOL!

Suppose that, although interest was shown, few said they'd be willing to buy one. At that point, rather than invest more money, I'd have cut my losses and looked for a new venture in some other field. The point is, even if you find a niche and give it all you've got, there is no guarantee you will win. On the other hand, as they say in the casinos, "You can't win if you don't play."

"Virtually nothing comes out right the first time," wrote the famous inventor Charles Kettering (1876–1958). "Failures, repeated failures, are finger posts on the road to achievement. The only time you don't fail is the last time you try something, and it works. One fails forward toward success."

Actually, if you enjoy what you're doing, why worry? "I would rather be a failure doing something I love," said the late comedian George Burns, "than be a success doing something I hate." I myself have been failing for years in the marine field, but it's something I love. Also, my plan is to "fail forward to success."

In 1971, I was set up to make the first east-to-west solo crossing of the Atlantic in an outboard motorboat. Winner Boats of Tennessee agreed to ship me a custom-built 22-footer; the Boston Whaler people promised three four-cycle Bearcat engines; and both the boat and the engines were to be mine once I'd made the crossing. I would take on fuel in Madeira, the Azores, and from the Coast Guard's Ocean Station vessel D.

Two letters arrived on the same day and shot me down. The first was from the Spanish government: import of *any* foreign boat was prohibited by law. No exceptions. The second letter was from the U.S. Coast Guard and went something like this: "We consider this to be too dangerous a trip. If, therefore, you show up at Ocean Station vessel D, we will pull you out of the water, and under no condition will we give you any fuel."

In 1975, I traveled all over North America looking for the world's best small planing boat with twin hulls because I considered small catamarans to be a niche market at that time. The search ended when I met Randy Kahn and Jeff Barr from Naples, Florida. They were just finishing a new fiberglass catamaran they called a SeaGull 14 (for the 14-foot length overall). I bought hull number one, along with a Honda 40, and hauled it on a trailer from Florida to Washington state. The local boat dealers wouldn't even consider the SeaGulls because they said catamarans lacked the "traditional" look so popular in the Northwest. (That viewpoint is slowly changing, by the way.)

Not one to give up easily, I made a deal with Washington's Skagit Orca Boats in 2001 to buy a demonstrator and equip it for a niche market. It would be the fastest little commercial cabin cruiser on the market, able to make the run from Seattle to Ketchikan in record-breaking time. On the very first trial out in Puget Sound, this 24-foot, deep-V-hulled, fully equipped cruiser with twin Evinrude 225s hit 60.2 miles an hour. Problem: At $119,000, it turned out to be too expensive compared to Bayliners (aka "Bumliners"). None of the locals would even make an offer, so to get rid of the boat, I advertised it on the Internet. I sold it at cost to a cop from Chicago.

One must press on. My next venture was to line up a million-dollar yacht, arrange to put it in the name of an LLC, and sell $50,000 memberships to 20 families in return for "ownership" two weeks of each year. Not a single taker, so *adios* yacht, but all I lost was some time and the small cost of some newspaper ads.

I like to think, however, that I am merely identifying things that—so far—do not work. Hope springs eternal. I already have my ticket to the next Boats Afloat Show in Vancouver, B.C. I'll be looking to create a new niche—something that no one could possibly need but that a select few might conceivably want.

In conclusion

Failure is not when you fall down. Failure is when you fail to get back up. As they say in Japan, "Fall seven times, get up eight." George Bernard Shaw was on the mark when he wrote, "A life spent making mistakes is not only more honorable, but more useful than a life spent doing nothing."

Nevertheless, a temporary failure may be only because you failed to find the correct angle or niche, or you failed to keep it simple. (Simplicity—to be discussed in detail in following chapter—is a key ingredient for success.) When you find or create the right niche, money will follow, and any previous failure will be just a distant memory!

AN EXAMPLE OF HOW TO CREATE A SIMPLE NICHE

A kind word and a SureFire are better than a kind word alone. – JJ Luna

If you don't already know what a SureFire flashlight is, go to www.surefire.com. Although the E2D Executive Defender is less than five inches long, it has a beam so bright that it can blind an attacker. That, along with its sharp scalloped edges at both ends, makes it one of the least-appreciated self-defense weapons anywhere. However, SureFires are sold internationally and are available on the Internet, so how could you create a simple niche?

One suggestion would be to take courses taught by martial artists known to be experts in the use of the Yawara Stick and the Kubotan (both of which are short cylinders similar in size to the Surefire E2D.) Then, apply what you learn to the use of the E2D. Your market will be the vast numbers of women who fear muggers and rapists. Teach them via seminars and individual classes. Prepare and sell a video and a small, illustrated book. Train others to become instructors in their own cities and states. Write magazine articles, appear on radio talk shows, and be quoted on television as THE expert in your chosen field.

The above is merely an example. Once you understand the principles involved, you can apply them to the field of your choice.

Suggested reading

Niche and Grow Rich, by Jennifer Basye Sander (Entrepreneur Press, 2003). This is the best single book on how to find a good idea for a niche market, how to develop it, and how to take it online. The author speaks from experience, having owned and operated several niche businesses, including gourmet coffee roasting, mail-order travel books, and a unique crafts business.

5
FOLLOW THE RULE OF "OCCAM'S RAZOR"

◆ ◆ ◆

Thus happiness depends, as Nature shows, Less on exterior things than most suppose. – English poet William Cowper

William of Occam (1284–1347) was an English philosopher and theologian who stressed the Aristotelian principle that "entities must not be multiplied beyond what is necessary." This principle became known as Occam's Razor. In the context of this book, it means that you must be on guard to not complicate your business or your life any more than is necessary.

For those of you who are overworked and overstressed, the solution may be to take the time to rethink what you are doing with your life. Consider the following experience.

The story of Elaine St. James

Back in 1990, Elaine St. James worked as many as 12 hours a day. She was a high-powered real estate investor, ran a thriving seminar business, and was the author of a popular book on real estate investing. Her sprawling country home, which required countless hours of upkeep, felt like a burden rather than a blessing. Her husband spent four hours a day commuting to the job that made it possible to live in that burdensome home. Eventually, however, St. James met with a career counselor who suggested she take a year off to figure out what she really wanted to do with her life.

"The suggestion was mind-boggling," she says. "My schedule wouldn't let me take a *day* off—let alone a year! But that suggestion, as crazy as it sounded at first, forced me to ask basic questions about my professional life. In fact, I did spend a year away from my job. And if I hadn't taken that time, I would have been in real estate forever."

Elaine St. James went on not only to simplify her life but to become one of the best-selling authors of books that emphasize living a simple life.

Never confuse simplicity with austerity

Even though you may have an abundant supply of money at present, or plan to acquire it in the future, you can still live in an unpretentious way and with an appreciation of simple things. Contrast this point of view with persons living in poverty who, if they ever came into a sudden windfall, would likely quit their jobs, buy a brand new luxury car, and spend, spend, spend until the money was gone. They would not only lose friends along the way but—as I've pointed out earlier—could end up more miserable than they were in the first place.

Simple living is never drab, never colorless. Watch young children at play. It is often the simple things that bring them joy long after the expensive toys are broken or forgotten.

How much is enough?

In the 1930s, my father ran a small general store near the Ontario-Minnesota border. Our rented home was 20x20 square feet. We lived without electricity, indoor plumbing, running water, central heating, and space. What we did have, however, was enough clothing to wear, good food to eat, a serviceable car, a party-line telephone, a radio, and an old wooden boat with a one-cylinder inboard engine. Since most of our neighbors had less, my sister and I always thought (correctly, for that time) that we were upper middle class. In fact, we had one precious commodity that even you may not currently have.

We had lots of free time.

After finishing my after-school chores, I had time to build model airplanes, conduct weird experiments (blowing up huge cardboard boxes filled with acetylene gas was a favorite), build a go-kart, go biking in the country, and read, read, read. The idea of buying some kind of name-brand clothing to wear to school never crossed the minds of any one of us. We all knew the maxims: Waste not, want not. A penny saved is a penny earned. A stitch in time saves nine.

Contrast that with the present generation. In Germany, according to an industrial research group, those between the ages of 14 and 24 in that country spend more than five billion euros a year on luxuries alone. In fact, to many young

Rhinelanders, the idea of thrift is a joke. In France, the goal of the majority is to dress in chic clothes, have a nice apartment, and drive a luxury sports car—these are the things that will give them *le standing*. Americans are not exempt from these desires, but Spain is worse. When we moved there in 1959, it was a paradise for our children and our children's friends. Today, however, most Spanish youths search in vain for happiness by going into debt for the latest fashions and sporty new cars.

Is this a goal you'd recommend to your children and to your grandchildren? If not, then why not live your life in such a way as to set an example for them to follow?

"Too many people," said the cowboy humorist Will Rogers, "spend money they haven't earned to buy things they don't want to impress people they don't like." Self-taught longshoreman philosopher Eric Hoffer wrote, "You can never get enough of what you don't need to make you happy." But Leonardo da Vinci said it best: *"Simplicity is the ultimate sophistication."*

For those of you in college

If you are currently enrolled in a university, here are a few suggestions to get you started on the road to a simpler and more satisfying life. (Some of these suggestions can be adjusted to those of you in other circumstances as well.)

- Never, never, never allow your peers to dictate what you should wear, who your friends should be, or how you

The Lunas at home in their apartment in Santa Cruz de Tenerife, 1964.

should live your life. (Peer pressure lessens every year, of course, and at my age, it is nonexistent.)

- Unless you are in a trade school, consider dropping out for at least a year. If you don't want to lose your friends, have them drop out with you. Pursue whatever it is you have a passion for. (What's just one year in a long life? If it doesn't work out, you can always go back.)
- Save time, money, and possible heartache during this time by never becoming involved with anyone you wouldn't want to marry. This includes but is not limited to potential mates who are addicts, unambitious, proud, selfish, miserly, cruel to animals, untruthful (even *once*), or who are already married to someone else.

"Straightforwardness and simplicity," wrote a Roman playwright, "are in keeping with goodness. The things that are essential are acquired with little bother; it is the luxuries that call for toil and effort." The author is Seneca, born in Spain 2000 years ago. China's Lao-Tzu, born nearly six centuries earlier than Seneca, has this to say: "To know you have enough is to be rich."

Simplicity when self-employed or starting a business

If you are (or plan to be) a carpenter, a plumber, a salesman, an artist, an architect, an accountant, or any similar profession where you *can* work alone, I suggest you *do* work alone. You may not get rich, but you can certainly shoot for at least $100,000 a year, and this will be sufficient if you live a simple, debt-free life.

In fact, the absolute best kinds of home-based businesses are those that can be run alone or just with help from family members. Many a small business, although successful in the beginning, has come to grief when the owner was tempted to expand. Business writer Michael LeBoeuf, in his book *The Perfect Business,* lists some of the problems connected with hiring one or more employees:

- Your freedom and flexibility will be forever restricted.
- You must give up privacy when an outsider comes into your home.
- You are now responsible for bringing in more money to cover wages and benefits.
- The government will burden you with odious payments and record-keeping chores.

- If an employee fails to show up for work, the extra work will either have to be done by you, or it won't get done at all.
- Every time someone quits, you have to start all over.

To the above, I would add one more caveat: Judging by what I read in the papers these days, if you have to fire a woman, she might come back to you with a charge of discrimination or harassment, and if you fire a man, he might come back with a gun.

Simplicity for any home-based business

Although the line between self-employment and having a home-based business is sometimes blurred, I consider a home-based business to be one that someone else could run. For example, here are a few of the one-person businesses that I've sold.

A photo mural business on Tenerife Island. I outlined to the buyer a simple system for making and mounting photo murals, gave him a list of all my clients, and signed a non-compete agreement.

An advertising specialty business in Montana. I instructed the buyer on how to set up appointments in advance with the use of direct mail. (No one else was doing this.) Also, I enabled him to buy directly from the manufacturers, thus doubling his commissions. He took over clients on my route, and I signed a non-compete agreement.

These small magnetic signs brought in many extra sales when the author sold advertising specialties in the Montana and Wyoming oil fields in 1983.

Forming Wyoming corporations for Europeans. I showed the buyer a simple method for forming the corporations and producing an attractive corporate kit. I then turned over my client list and signed a non-compete agreement.

Each of the above was a "blue sky" sale. That is, few if any tangible assets were included. What each buyer did receive was a system for doing business, a list of clients that I had built up from scratch, and a non-compete agreement. None of the buyers had to spend a dollar on advertising because all future business came from repeat orders and word-of-mouth.

My current income consists of (1) royalties from my *How to Be Invisible* book, (2) profit from self-publishing this book,

(3) occasional fees of up to $500 an hour as a consultant, (4) 1 percent per month interest from short-term real estate loans, and (5) finder's fees from an anonymous information-based Internet business.

Note the simplicity. With the exception of self-publishing, none of the above takes up much of my time. The last one, in fact, requires less than an hour a day and yet is doing so well that I could find a dozen buyers for it within a week. (However, please do not contact me for details. This one is a keeper.)

Short-term complications vs. long-term simplicity

Your strategic goal should always be to simplify your life. If that complicates your life in the short run, pay the price. Apply the principle of Occam's Razor, and reap the eventual benefits in your family, your business, and your life.

Raising children. Read to them and with them from the time they are born. Care for them yourselves—no babysitters, no day-care centers, no television, no video games. Teach them from the cradle that "no" means "no," and back this up with spanking and/or a loss of privileges. This is hard work, parents, but it may immeasurably simplify your problems when the kids reach puberty.

Paying cash and building an emergency fund. If you are presently in debt, you may have to do some serious suffering before you break free and then build up a cash fund for emergencies. But after that, life can be simple and sweet. No more monthly payments on debt. No more worries about a sudden loss of income. And if you are renting from month to month and suddenly decide to make a move, how simple that will be!

Starting a new business. In the beginning, you may suffer from worry, stress, and overwork. Press on. In the long run, your life can be as simple as you care to make it. You'll have extra time when you need it, extra cash when you want it, and will never again have to worry about being laid off, fired, or having to work under the lash of a tyrannical boss.

Buying new things. Before you buy any more furniture, clothing, stereos, TVs, tools, ornaments or whatever, remember that in addition to working more hours to pay for the new purchase, it is also going to take up space and take up time—time to install, move, dust, maintain, listen to, look at, clean, or fix. Before you buy *anything*, first ask yourself if this is going to simplify your life.

Concluding observations about keeping things simple

- If you start a new business, start it alone or with others in your family, but never with an outside partner.
- If, like me, you like to mess about in boats, buy one small enough to be handled by a single person. (I could write a book about the pros and cons of buying a boat. Someday I may.)
- When you rent, purchase, or build a home, limit the size so that outside help is seldom needed. (No room

for guests? Send them to a motel and pay the bill—this is much cheaper than paying for a bigger house or apartment!)

Do not, of course, oversimplify. Find a balance. Cars need spare tires, offshore boats need life rafts, and small businesses need backup plans or equipment. You'll learn more about this in the next chapter.

SIMPLIFY, SIMPLIFY, SIMPLIFY

- *Before making any major decision, ask yourself this question:* "If I do thus-and-so, will it simplify my life?"
- *Self-employment and starting a business:* Keep it small, and keep it simple.
- *Of special interest to high school students:* Attending a university and perhaps going into debt with student loans may not simplify your life. Discuss this with your parents.

Suggested reading

Million Dollar Habits, by Robert J. Ringer (Wynwood, 1990). Ringer discusses simplicity, attitude, perspective, morality, human relations, and self-discipline, all in a commonsense way that can help anyone improve. *Highly recommended!*

6
HOW TO DO BUSINESS LIKE A PRO

◆ ◆ ◆

Let your 'Yes' mean 'Yes,' and your 'No' mean 'No.'
– Matthew 5:37

Although some of you may have heard this story about the contractor's advice to his son, others may have missed it, so I include it here.

"Son," says the father, "when you start your own business, I want you to follow two rules. The first one is, when you set a date for completion, you must honor that date. It doesn't matter if a storm comes through, or if the workers strike, or if you break a leg, or if the country goes to war. Complete the job on schedule, even if it takes you into bankruptcy."

"Yes, Father. And the second rule?"

"Never set a date."

I think I met that son when our last house was built. The general contractor told us that we would probably move in by the end of the year. Then he said February. Then April. The actual completion date turned out to be June. Now, the contractor was an honest man. He had some good ideas for changes as we went along. His price was reasonable. In fact, everything was fine except for the finishing date, but because of this, would I recommend him to a friend? Nope. Not even for a doghouse.

Suppose, on the other hand, that the contractor had given us a completion date of July of the following year. Then, when we moved in a month early, we'd have been delighted!

Set a date, but set it late

With one exception, I have always met, and often beat, my promised deadlines. The secret is simple. I set a date *beyond* the expected completion date, and if the customer doesn't like that, I turn down the business.

A young woman in Ohio, Kitty McMenemy, takes orders for the New Mexico limited liability companies (LLCs) that I recommend for hiding ownership of vehicles and real estate. New customers often request "fast service," but her order blanks clearly state that the average turnaround time for the legal documents is up to five weeks. She follows my instructions to turn down any order where the customer wants the documents sooner.

In actual practice, the law in New Mexico states that LLCs must be filed and sent back to the organizer within 15 business days. Sometimes they do it in a week, sometimes they use the entire time allotted, and once in awhile—*law or no law*—they take 20 business days (about 25 calendar days). But the customer always gets his documents within five weeks, and most of the time in less. Result? Happy clients who recommend her services to their friends. In conclusion:

If you say "yes," then *do* it.
Otherwise, just say "no."

Tell the truth: No spin, no exaggeration

In the Canary Islands, as well as in Malaga and Barcelona, the major bazaars that sell imported luxury goods are run by immigrants from India. They all know one another because they've all come from the same small area in their mother country and, in fact, many are related. They all lie. The locals know that and learn to live with it, but they don't like it. One of my acquaintances in Santa Cruz de Tenerife was Kishu Mahtani, who owned and ran Bazaar Kishu near Plaza de España back in the 1970s. I used to urge him to tell the truth to his customers, but his answer was, "We don't just lie to the customers, we lie to *each other*. If I didn't do whatever the others do, I'd go broke in a week!"

Some years later, a friend in Barcelona told me about an owner of a bazaar in that city who decided to tell the truth. The only reason he did so was that he had become disgusted with his own religion and had started to study the Bible with my friend. It soon became obvious that if he were to progress, the lying had to stop, even if it meant the end of his business. And yes, in the beginning, there was a drop in sales. But slowly, steadily, the word spread among the locals that the bazaar on so-and-so street was the place to go because it was run by an "honest Indian!" In less than a year, his business nearly doubled.

I run my little businesses by telling the truth, and I urge you to do the same. You may lose some sales, especially in the beginning, but in the long run, honesty is not only the best way, it is the *only* way.

The difference between an amateur and a pro

An amateur usually completes the job as promised and on time. The professional *always* does so. Whichever field you enter, plan beforehand on what your backup plan will be when an emergency arises because—trust me on this one!—*an emergency will eventually arise.*

Photography. When I worked as a wedding photographer for high society in the Canary Islands, I did something that no other photographer did: I taught a local girl, Nancy Hernandez, to work along with me and shoot the same pictures I was shooting, but from the opposite side of the altar. I furnished her with a camera and flash units identical to my own. Back in the darkroom, I first developed my own films so that if an error was made in processing, I had her rolls of film as backup.

On one memorable occasion, I was shooting the wedding of a small-town mayor's daughter in the elegant 15th-century cathedral up in La Laguna. When the time came for the groom to slip the ring on the finger of his bride, which is the crowning moment in any Spanish wedding, I don't know what happened—if the shutter malfunctioned or the flash failed or what—but *I missed the picture*. I shot a pained look at Nancy, who responded with a wink, a nod, and a smile that said *I got it*. I delivered a professionally-done album to my clients, and they recommended me to their friends.

Consulting. Although emergencies seldom arise, occasionally a client will need some advice and will send me an urgent e-mail, expecting a very fast answer. Therefore, even though I am traveling, I am always able to respond. Suppose, however, that the computer I use for e-mail broke down? No problem, because I travel with *two* laptops: an IBM ThinkPad and a Sony Vaio. Both have long-life batteries, and both are equipped for wireless.

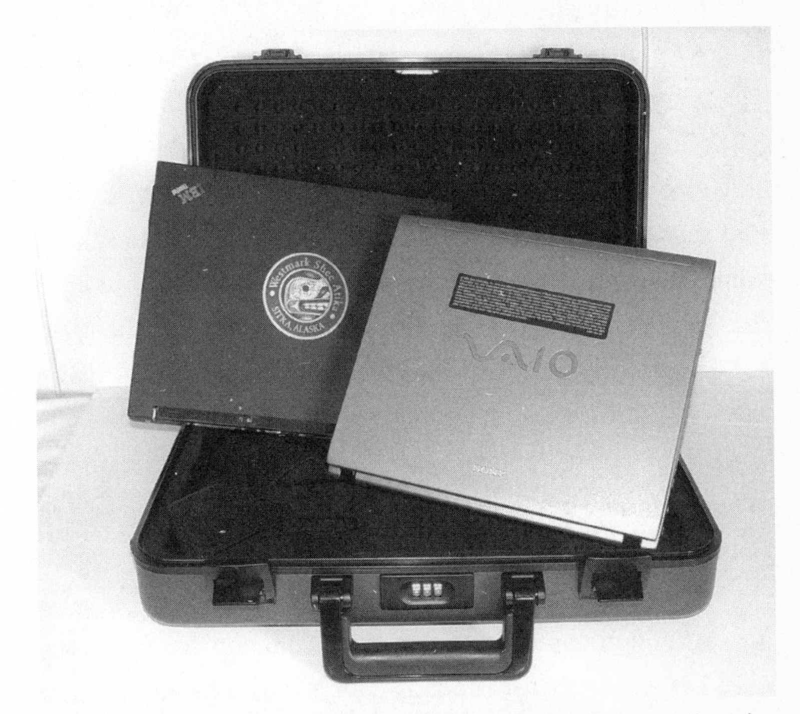

According to the author, a true professional never fails to get the job done, which often entails duplicate equipment. He, therefore, carries two laptops when he travels in case one should fail for any reason.

Learn from a bad example. For a commercial example of an amateur operation, take any McDonald's franchise. They may be professionals in every other way, but they are rank amateurs when it comes to selling ice cream cones. Without exaggeration, I have patiently edged along various drive-thru lines more than 30 times to get an ice cream cone, only to learn that no cones are available. Here are some of the pathetic excuses:

- The machine is broken.
- We forgot to turn the machine on.
- The machine is down for cleaning. (This is often on Monday morning.)
- The ice cream is too soft (because of making many cones in a short time).

One solution would be to have a sign prepared in advance that says, "Sorry, no ice cream at this time," and stick it up where it would be seen before one entered the drive-thru lane. The correct solution, however, would be to require two ice cream machines in every franchise, no exceptions. (Are you listening, McDonald's?)

When you absolutely, positively need something done, go to the top

Although this would seem to be common sense, experience has shown that it is not as common as it should be, so I include two examples of how this works.

Photography. My success in getting the top weddings on Tenerife Island did not go unnoticed by the local photographers. They waited until I was shooting a spectacular wedding in the Church of the Conception—twin brides were marrying two brothers—and then made their move. At the moment that the two couples stepped up to the altar, the police shot out from a side entrance and arrested me in front of the entire congregation! As they led me down the aisle, the local photographers took over my job.

At the police station, I learned that the charge was "running a business without a license." (The locals assumed that since I was a foreigner, I was no doubt working illegally.) Surprise! I not only had my permanent residence in order, along with a license to work in the province, I even had a Santa Cruz *city* license. Not even the locals had bothered to obtain that one, since it was quite expensive!

That got me back on the street, but the problem with the local photographers remained, so it was time to go to the top. In 1963, the "top" was not the chief of police, the mayor, or even the governor general of the islands. It was the Catholic bishop. Talk about Daniel going into the lion's den! I was one of the bishop's arch enemies (along with my good friend Antonio Rodriguez from northern Spain) because we were secretly conducting Bible-study meetings in both private homes and in large meetings deep in the heart of the island's mountain forests. The bishop knew *something* was going on, and had ordered the secret police to find out who was behind this and put a stop to it. In fact, an alert had just gone out on the island radio to beware of a "foreigner known as Ricardo."

Known only as "Ricardo," the author is seen speaking to more than a hundred persons deep in a mountain forest. In 1963, Spanish law prohibited any meeting of 20 or more persons, as well as any religious meeting not sanctioned by the Catholic Church. Although many of his friends were caught and jailed, the author eluded the secret police until 1970, when the laws were changed to permit religious liberty.

However, since the bishop had no way of knowing that I was Ricardo, I took Nancy with me and went to see him to resolve the problem with the local photographers. When we entered his ornate office in Las Laguna, he extended his hand with the palm down, displaying a large ring on one of his fingers, but I reached around and shook his hand. (Nancy later told me that he expected me to kneel and kiss the ring. In this case, ignorance was bliss.) I explained my recent arrest, the results that had followed, and that, like everyone else on the island, I had a family to feed. He nodded and said he would send down word to allow me to "*trabajar como Dios manda*" (to work as God commands). When we stood up to leave, he smiled and offered me his hand in the normal way.

As bishops go, this was one of the good guys. Never again did I have a problem with the local photographers.

Incorporating. Before I started forming corporations in Wyoming, I called the state capitol in Cheyenne and asked to be put through to Kathy Karpan, the Secretary of State. (This approach works better in small-population states, of course, than it would in New York or California.) When someone named Margy White took the call, I explained that before I started sending them an unusually large amount of business, I'd like to take the Secretary of State out to lunch.

"It's election time," she said, "and Kathy is out on the campaign trail. But I'm the Deputy Secretary of State, in charge while she's away, so will I do?"

I was on the plane to Cheyenne the next day. Margy brought another woman with her—the head of corporations—and we had a memorable meal at Little America. From that moment on, if any problem came up or some favor was needed, all I had to do was call Margy.

Wait long, strike fast

When the time comes to strike, strike fast. If there is any trick to this, it is to learn when to wait and when to strike. Two examples follow—one for buying, the other for selling—but remember: The principles apply to many different situations.

Buying. If you can afford to wait, then wait until the time is right. Last year, my wife and I decided to search for a certain Lincoln Town Car in first-class condition. It had to be a 1997 because that was the last year that Lincoln produced the full-sized model, and we liked the style. I watched the classified ads for months before spotting an ad for a low-mileage one-owner 1997. This was in the Sunday edition of a newspaper in a nearby city, and it was the first time the ad had appeared. I called the number, talked to a man named Gene who was selling the car, and asked if he would consider a discount for immediate sale. He said yes, so I arranged to meet him within two hours. When I arrived, Gene said several others had called, but I was the first to arrive. The light blue Lincoln was a cream puff, just what we'd been looking for. (It belonged to this man's father, whose wife had just died. The old car held too many memories, so the son bought him a new Lincoln and was now selling this one.) Another prospective buyer drove up just as we were about to go for a test drive.

"Please wait," said Gene. "We're going for a little drive, but I'll be right back."

Within four blocks I knew that this was what I'd been looking for, so I pulled over to the curb and said I'd buy it.

"Well . . . I know I said on the phone that I'd allow you a discount, but since there are some others that still want to see it . . ."

"No problem. I will pay your full asking price."

"Oh. Well, of course, since this is Sunday, the banks—"

"I brought the cash."

"You did?"

The car was mine.

Selling. Early one morning in the spring of 1959, when I was still in the outdoor sign business, I pulled into a new independent gas station that had just opened in Rugby, North Dakota. (Trivia item: Rugby is the geographical center of North America.) The owner already had a sign on order, but he thought a friend of his down in Sheridan, Wyoming, was still shopping for one.

"Would you mind calling him and letting me talk to him, please?" I asked. The man did indeed need a sign and had already been discussing it with a local sign shop. I said I'd like to see him the next day.

"What time?" he asked.

"What time do you come down to the station?"

"Seven o'clock."

"I will be there at seven sharp."

It was a 600-mile drive, which meant I had to take off immediately. I stopped along the way only for gas, snacks, and once to sleep for a few hours in the car. And yes, I sold the sign, but only because I got down there with lightning speed.

Speed alone is not, of course, the entire story. Neither is the first impression. But if the first impression is poor, the speed will have been wasted and the rest of the story will never be told. Creating the right kind of first impression is, therefore, the topic of the following chapter.

DO BUSINESS LIKE A TRUE PROFESSIONAL

- Always have a backup plan in place.
- Set dates far enough ahead so that you can deliver ahead of schedule.
- When you need help, aim high. Can you take someone to lunch?
- When necessary, wait long, but be prepared to strike fast.

Suggested reading

The Perfect Business: How to Make a Million From Home with No Payroll, No Debts, No Employee Headaches, and No Sleepless Nights! by Michael LeBoeuf (Simon & Schuster, 1996.) The title is misleading; the book does not describe a perfect business. Nevertheless, this is an excellent self-help guide because it distills the best ideas of the countless success manuals written over the past 100 years and applies this philosophy to the field of self-employment.

7
MAKE A POWERFUL FIRST IMPRESSION

◆ ◆ ◆

You never get a second chance to make a first impression. – *Anonymous*

I used to thumb my way across the country and beat the Greyhound bus schedule every time, passing all those scraggly hitchhikers who were stuck in the same place for hours on end. Here was the secret of my success. I was:

1. Standing straight, right arm out at a downward angle, thumb pointing ahead.
2. Clean-shaven and had a short haircut.
3. Wearing pressed trousers, a clean white shirt, and a red necktie.
4. Carrying a neat leather attaché case in my left hand.

The only reason that drivers picked me up was because they received a favorable impression within the first three seconds. That basic truth carries over into every profession, every business, every relationship. It applies to the quality of your smile, the cut of your hair, the shine on your shoes, the paint on your home, the breed of your dog, the words you use, and in some cases, even the make and model of the vehicle you drive.

A never-ending assignment for homework

One of your main keys to success in any field will be to constantly analyze first impressions by sight, sound, smell, and context. If your impression was good, why was it good? If your impression was bad, why was it bad?

Are you a single man, about to meet a blind date for lunch? What if she's a looker but reeks of cheap perfume? Are you an older woman, searching for a suitable nursing home for your 90-year-old mother? What if, as you enter an attractive nursing home, you get a whiff of stale urine in the air? In either situation, your initial impression comes from a single source: smell. In the case of a hitchhiker, the initial impression also comes from a single source: appearance.

As you watch for good and bad impressions, think how best to imitate the good ones. Make mental notes as to how the bad ones could have been corrected. Here are some ideas to get you started:

- As you drive up to someone's home, what is your first overall impression? Does your impression change as you stand before the entrance door? What do you see when you look into the kitchen?

- Check the ads in the Yellow Pages for pet shops, plumbers or pest control. If you had to call someone fast about a dog, a water leak, or an insect infection, which company would you call?
- On your next visit to the dentist or doctor, look around the waiting room. Is it clean and neat, with comfortable chairs, live plants, good lighting, and with current magazines? What kind of pictures or charts are on the wall? If this were your office, how would you improve it?
- The next time you're in traffic and stopped for a red light, look around for a van or a pickup with signs on the sides. Is this a vehicle that you would choose if you had that business? Are the signs both attention-getting and easy to read? Is an easy-to-remember Web site prominently listed? (Did a horn just sound behind you? Observe that the traffic light is now green.)
- When you sort out the day's mail, which envelope will be the first you open, and why? If the last one you open is just an advertisement, look closely at the cover letter before you throw it away. Are you greeted by your name? Is there a signature? A short P.S. that follows?
- Keep an eye out for business uniforms—painters, mechanics, maids, waitresses, whatever. Check for color, style, and fit. Is the uniform clean and neat? Does it fit the service?
- Start watching heads when you are out and about. Do you like that young woman's heavy makeup, dyed hair, or her three-inch dangling earrings? How about that young man with a ponytail? Are you impressed

by the triangle of hair under his lower lip? His sleeveless-shirt? Or the tattoo of barbed wire around his right bicep?

- Check out the clothing of persons of your own sex. Imagine yourself dressed the same way, right down to the shoes. If you were in business, would your customers be impressed? If not, what would have to be changed?
- If a stranger pulled into your driveway with a late-model Jaguar, what kind of person would you expect to step out? What if the car were a Ford Escort instead of a Jaguar?
- If you have an e-mail account, analyze the incoming messages and the addresses of the senders. *Within six seconds*, which of these names impresses you more: freakybaby@hotmail.com or BrookeBarrington@MontanaTeddyBears.com? Does the subject line match the message? Is there a salutation? How does the sender sign off? Would the punctuation pass muster with Lynne Truss, author of *Eats, Shoots & Leaves*?
- We live in an age where almost *any* business needs a Web site. Run a search on Google. Use a key phrase for a field of business that you yourself might wish to enter. If you have a dial-up connection, count the seconds it takes to load the page. How much time goes by before you quit waiting and move on? If the page does come up quickly, is it simple and easy to read, with the key points in boldface? Are the links intuitive, or do you bumble around the site in trial and error?

- Go to a bookstore. Check out a section where—if you became a writer—your book might be shelved. Which book covers jump out at you, and why?
- On your next trip along a state highway, pay attention to the billboards. Which ones are easiest to read? To keep the kids from asking if you're there yet, start a contest to see who can first find a sign that has just seven words or less. (More than seven is often too many.) Or look for a sign that needs paint. Or a sign that's just plain *dumb*.

A few lessons learned from my own home-based businesses

Show rather than tell. When I walked into the office of an architect or a hotel director for the first time, I carried—and then held up—one of my most spectacular seacoast scenes. *Then* I said hello and shook hands.

Respond with blinding speed. The moment a fax started to come through from Europe with a request for information about Wyoming corporations, I was ready with a form letter on the screen. I raced to add the sender's name, personalized it in some way, printed it out, and faxed it back. The customer had my answer within three minutes or less. One woman from Austria responded, "When I send you a question, and the answer appears in my fax almost as soon as I've finished sending it, it seems like *magic*!"

In direct mail campaigns, the first objective is to make sure each envelope is opened. Envelopes such as the one shown above are *always* opened!

Make sure your letters are opened and read. Even when my wife and I were once mailing 2,000 letters a week, every letter carried a first-class commemorative stamp and was personally signed with a blue felt-tip pen. In other cases, when I wished to draw attention to an important letter, I used an ivory-colored 6x9-inch envelope with at least five very old commemorative stamps that I purchased from a stamp dealer at face value. I then used a rubber stamp to apply a detailed red eagle on the left, and I added a blue "filed" stamp over the base of the eagle, and inserted the date. A little too jazzy? Maybe . . . but I've been told more than once that such letters were opened ahead of all others.

Jazz up the documents. If you've ever had a law firm prepare Articles of Incorporation, you know that they just use lined or plain paper. However, the first thing my European clients saw when they opened the FedEx envelope were the Wyoming Articles of Incorporation printed on heavy all-cotton bond paper with an engraved blue border and a gold seal at the bottom, embossed with the name of the incorporator.

Demonstrate the product. About 55 years ago, I spent a year selling revolving amber beacons to bars and cafés that were scattered along winding state highways in the rural areas of Montana and North Dakota. When I entered the premises carrying the good-looking beacon with a chromed base, I went straight for an outlet and plugged in the beacon. Only when it was revolving and flashing did I explain to the owner that for $95, this little item would increase his business from the very moment it was mounted outside. Which—until later outlawed by the state patrol—it definitely did.

Never discount without a reason that is immediately evident. When I was demonstrating the beacons, the business owner would sometimes say he couldn't afford the $95 unit. I would answer, "I've got another beacon out in the car, the same as this one, but with a little dent in the base. If you don't mind the dent, you can have it for $65." No one ever minded a little dent in return for a $30 discount, so I'd take the beacon out to my car, open the trunk, give the base a whack with a ball peen hammer, and bring the same beacon back in. I sold a lot

Application for a Canary Islands street address

All annual prices are in euros (€). The present exchange rate fluctuates between $1.40 and $1.45.

Date: ___________.

By submitting this application, I declare that I have read and agree with the instructions listed separately. I understand that the yearly fees for forwarding up to 12, 25, or 50 letters per year are as listed below and that if many additional letters are received, my annual rate will increase.

Introductory setup fee, including one name for mail forwarding: **$195**

Option: ________ **additional** names, @ $50 per name: $_____

==========

SUBTOTAL: $________

Add for the first year:

- ☐ Up to 12 letters per year, €120 ($175) ________
- ☐ Up to 25 letters per year, €200 ($290) ________
- ☐ Up to 50 letters per year, €350 ($500) ________

TOTAL ENCLOSED **$________**

Please send my new Canary Islands address to:

Name: ______________________________

Address: ______________________________

____

☐ PLEASE CONFIRM RECEIPT OF THIS ORDER:

E-mail ____________ @ ____________

Option: My telephone number is: ____________ (in case of any questions.)

Limited offer, good until September 30

Be sure to fill out the DATA SHEET on the reverse side

The author invariably uses bond paper with engraved borders to make that vital first impression for all order or application blanks.

of dented beacons in those days, but since my wholesale cost was only $35, it was still a good business.

In conclusion

Whatever your future business may be, never forget to constantly monitor the first impression. Although a favorable first impression is not a guarantee of success, an unfavorable impression will almost certainly spell failure.

- *Direct mail*: If the envelope appears to be an advertisement, it may go straight into the wastebasket without ever being opened.
- *Inquiries*: If you fail to answer an e-mail or return a telephone called promptly, the sender or the caller may well look elsewhere for your product or service.
- *Business vehicle:* If your business requires a van, for example, the van should have an excellent paint job, be kept clean on the outside, and free from clutter on the inside. (I once saw a van for a cleaning service. On the dash were the wrappings of a hamburger, an opened package of cigarettes, and an empty beer can . . .)

Maintain a low profile

I prefer not to stand out in my neighborhood nor to draw the attention of any agent of the city, county, state, or federal government. After reading the next chapter about flying beneath the radar, you may decide to do a little low-level flying yourself.

CONSTANTLY MONITOR FIRST IMPRESSIONS

- Start analyzing at once the first impression you get from meeting new people, reading new signs, and going new places. Consider appearance, sound, smell, feel, touch, and/or taste.
- When you go into business for yourself, prepare in advance the way in which you or your product will make a favorable impact within the first few seconds.
- Never cut the price of your product or service without giving a reason that makes immediate good sense, e.g., it is outdated, leftover, or damaged in some way. *Dent the beacon*.

Suggested reading

You've Only Got Three Seconds: How to Make the Right Impression in Your Business and Social Life, by Camille Lavington and Stephanie Losee (Doubleday, 1998). Although this book is aimed primarily at those in the corporate world, it contains gems that fit perfectly with a one-person business.

How to Make a Million Dollar First Impression, by Lynda Goldman (Goldman Smythe Business Class, 2000). You'll find 105 new ideas packed into this 164-page book—especially for those in sales or in customer service. The author emphasizes the basic impressions made when you contact a prospective customer in person or by e-mail, letter, phone, or fax.

8
HOW TO FLY BENEATH THE RADAR

◆ ◆ ◆

Do not, as long as you live, ever again allow your real name to be coupled with your home address. – *J. J. Luna*

A few years ago, when I was away on a trip, my wife received a phone call on her cell phone that would have terrified many women staying alone. The call came from a close relative who bore a strong resemblance to Charles Manson, so I'll refer to him as Charlie. Charlie had just learned what my wife had said about him when she wrote to another person, and he had taken extreme offense. So extreme, in fact, that he said he was preparing to fly west to see us. "I'm going to kill you [expletive deleted] and then burn your place down with you two in it!"

This was no idle threat. Charlie had driven his first wife to suicide and his second wife lived in terror. Furthermore, Charlie was a pilot, he owned his own plane, and since he was retired, he had the time to carry out his plan.

If you had received a similar phone call, how would you react? What steps would—or *could*—you take to protect yourself?

Although my wife didn't appreciate the call, she knew something that Charlie did not. The address he had for us was in another town, and the house, the cell phone, and the utilities were all in other names. Our vehicles were untraceable, and our driver's licenses were from another state. In short, my wife knew that as far as Charlie was concerned, *we were invisible.*

Don't tell me that you've got nothing to fear. Neither have countless others—especially those with home-based businesses—who later fell victim to disgruntled customers, ex-lovers, stalkers, or freaks.

I have never had a problem with this, but perhaps it is because my customers and clients never know where I live. This is a course of action that I recommend to you. Even though you may prefer not to pursue privacy to my level, I urge you to consider the following basic steps.

Hide your home address

This means, first and foremost, that you will stop receiving mail or deliveries of any kind at your home. At the very least, rent a box at a Commercial Mail Receiving Agency (CMRA). These can be found in the Yellow Pages under categories such as MAILBOXES—RETAIL and MAILBOX RENTAL & RECEIVING. If given a choice, choose a small mom-and-pop service because they are more private than the big chains such as PostNet and The UPS stores. You may also wish to use a P.O. box for normal business mail, but you'll still need the CMRA for non-postal services such as UPS, FedEx, and the various other courier services.

True, both the postal service and the CMRAs will require a picture ID, and this in turn will usually reveal your present home address, but at least your new CMRA address will not lead directly to where you live. (Private investigators can sometimes get your true address through these two agencies, legally or otherwise. The only protection against this possibility is to move and neglect to update your old address.)

Many readers of *How to Be Invisible* have gone to the extra work of obtaining what I call a "ghost" address: a street address with no additional telltale box number that immediately tells others it is not your true address. The difference is obvious:

Ghost address:	1776 Washington Avenue
CMRA address:	1776 Washington Avenue, #123

Some have even obtained ghost addresses in such places as unused office buildings, broom closets, small motels, and with paralegal and bookkeeping services.

Keep your telephone number from revealing your home address

If you require a land line, at the very least make sure it is unlisted, unpublished, has call blocking, and is listed in another name. (Note: Do not then use this line to call a toll-free number because such numbers capture your name and number with Automatic Number Identification (ANI). These "captures" are often then sold to Internet companies who, in turn, sell this information to the public.)

If you are a married woman, you can sometimes list your telephone in your maiden name. In other cases, as long as you show your true identity to a telephone company representative, you will be allowed to subscribe in an alternate name, perhaps that of a man.

The same is true for obtaining cable TV, and in this case you may wish to add an Internet telephone service (Voice over Internet Protocol, or VoIP) from a company such as Vonage (www.vonage.com). Thus you can eliminate the land line altogether.

More commonly, you can obtain a cell phone (prepaid if necessary) without revealing where you live, and this may be the best solution. In fact, an expert in the field tells me that within eight years, land line telephones may disappear entirely, replaced by cell phones and VoIP.

Hide your real estate and vehicle ownership

This one's easy. Title the name of each asset in the name of a trust or in the name of a New Mexico limited liability company. Use a ghost address in Alaska (or, if you live there, use an address in the Lower 48).

Open your bank account elsewhere

There is no easy solution to this one, but wherever you bank, make sure that the bank does not have your home address or land line telephone number. (If you do have a land line, give them your cell phone number. If you do not have a cell phone, get a cheap pager and give them that number.) For the best results, consider opening your account in a small, privately owned bank in another state, one that does not border your own state.

Do not use an ATM or a credit card with this account. Reason: In the United States, anyone can sue anyone else for virtually any reason whatsoever. However, before taking a case against you, a lawyer will normally have a private investigator (PI) run an asset check first. This is to make sure that you have "deep pockets," i.e., enough assets to make the lawsuit worthwhile. The PI will check for vehicles, real estate, stocks, bonds, credit cards, ATM withdrawals, *and bank accounts* in your name. He will expect this bank account to be in the same state where you are doing business and that it will be tied in with the use of a credit card.

If the initial search fails, the PI may then start checking the bordering states. If at this point no substantial assets have appeared, the lawyer will most likely call the search to a halt and decline to take the case.

The ultimate solution. Perhaps you have a trusted friend from another state who is willing to help you for a reasonable fee. Let's say her name is Sally. Have her open a non-interest-bearing account in her own name. (Follow the same procedure as above with regard to hiding her true home address and telephone number.) She will order a certain number of checks. When these arrive, she will sign all the checks and then turn them over to you. Then, whenever you write a check, you merely fill out the amount and the payee. As for bank deposits, use the usual rubber stamp that says "For Deposit Only," followed by the account number and Sally's name or initials. Mail them in.

A business name may not be necessary for your bank account. A personal account will be far more private. Have checks made payable to either an initial and a last name, or—even better—to three initials only. In the latter case, open the personal account with two initials and a last name, such as P.D. Quigley, and make sure that a check made out to just P.D.Q. may be deposited with no problem. If you really want to be cute, use a business name that has the same three initials as either yours or Sally's. Example:

Name of the nominee:	Sally Louise Smith (S.L.S.)
Name on the bank account:	S. L. Smith
Name of the business:	Silver Lake Services (S.L.S.)

Have your checks printed the same way: three initials at the upper left, no address. And have the numbers start with 4001 or higher, so it looks to your customers as if you've had the account for a long time.

Create an invisible owner for your business

Such "owners" are invisible because *they do not exist.* Unless fraud is involved, I believe this practice to be entirely legal. Let's suppose your name is Carmen M. Chavez, Golda A. Goldstein, or Bashiyra Binte Nur Um Lifti. You decide to start a business via the Internet, and you decide that, in the particular field you have chosen, a generic-type man's name would look better.

First, choose a three-word business name with the same initials as yours. Then invent a man's name with the same initials. For example:

Your actual name:	Carmen M. Chavez
Bank account name:	C. M. Chavez
Business name:	Custom Made Canes
"Owner" name:	Curt M. Caldwell
Checks made out to:	C.M.C.

The opposite is true, of course, if you are a man who wishes to sell merchandise that will appeal to women. Choose a woman's name that will seem best to go with the product.

Bad advice from how-to-start-your-own-business books

Here is a list of recommended things to do before you start your business, taken from a number of books written by so-called experts in the field. The recommendations are in italics. My personal and highly subjective comments follow.

- ◆ *Call your city or county government to check zoning rules because your neighborhood may have restrictions.*
  - Don't ask, don't tell.

- ◆ *Decide if you will be incorporated. Talk to a lawyer.*
  - Skip the lawyer. Do not incorporate. Later, you may wish to use a limited liability company, but even there, a lawyer may be of no help. Many are unfamiliar with their proper use, and not one in a hundred will even *think* of recommending New Mexico for maximum privacy.

- ◆ *If you will be in a partnership or have employees, obtain an Employer's Identification Number (EIN) through the IRS. Also, if you have employees, call the Employment Commission for information on unemployment taxes you must pay.*
  - Do not enter into a partnership. Do not get an EIN. Do not take on a single employee. Later, if you MUST have help, use an LLC with each worker as a member, and spell it all out in an operating agreement. There will be tax consequences, so choose this route only when working with an enrolled agent or a CPA.

- ◆ *Register your business name. Contact your county courthouse.*

    - Do not contact anyone in your state. Use your own name or initials, or—if you must—file for a business name in some other state, perhaps the one where your personal bank account is.

- *Obtain any state or federal licenses, if required by your business.*
    - I suggest you simply never enter any field that requires a state or federal license.

- *Set up your business checking accounts.*
    - No! Use a *personal* account for business, and keep it out of state.

- *Obtain a separate business telephone line.*
    - No again! In my own recent businesses, I've never given out a telephone number at all. All orders arrived via e-mail, normal mail, and FedEx. If you do need a number, make it that of a pager, a cell phone, or Voice over Internet Protocol (VoIP).

- *Order business stationery and cards.*
    - Don't order either one. You can print letterheads on your own inkjet printer, and there are usually better ways to advertise than with a business card. Try a colored postcard, a booklet, or hand the prospect your self-published book! (In quantity, you can get a 64-page book for about 98 cents a copy. Did you know that?)

- *Develop a detailed business plan.*
    - I have never developed a business plan in my life. Those who do develop them usually change or abandon them as soon as things get under way. The primary use of a business plan is to get financing from a bank or from a venture capitalist, but you are going to start out on a cash basis—*right, Bunky?*

The problem with spending four years in a business school

Such an education may require time and money that could better be used in the actual experience of starting and running one or more home-based businesses. A street-smart business-oriented education, gained by doing battle in the arena, will stay with you as long as you live. The next chapter, therefore, is dedicated to a discussion of a formal education versus a street-smart education.

ADDITIONAL TIPS FOR PERSONAL PRIVACY

- Do not give your Social Security number to anyone other than a state or federal agency that requires it.
- Either do not use a middle initial, or else use your middle name with no first initial. (The idea is to blend your name in with those who have the same name.)
- Do not give out your correct date of birth. (It is used to identify you almost as easily as if you gave out your Social Security number.)

- Never, ever give out your true home address. Not to your dentist. Not to your doctor. Not to the butcher, the baker, or the candlestick maker.
- Never, ever show your driver's license to anyone other than a police officer who stops you for a traffic offense. For all other requests for identification—at the bank, the post office, or the airport—show your passport only. (If you do not yet have a passport, obtain one at once. Unlike a driver's license, a passport does not show any address whatsoever, not even your state, and (as of this writing, at least) it lacks other information as well—especially the information contained on those new magnetic strips now appearing on many new driver's licenses.)

Suggested reading

How to Be Invisible: The Essential Guide to Protecting Your Personal Privacy, Your Assets, and Your Life, Revised Edition, by J.J. Luna (St. Martin's Press, 2004). In addition to the information found in this section, the book has chapters on repairmen, untraceable trash, alternate names and signatures, how to find and use nominees, e-mails and the Internet, money transfers, anonymous utilities, and how to use limited liability companies.

Some of the overflow from Luna's eclectic library of more than a thousand books.

9
FORMAL VS. STREET-SMART EDUCATION

◆ ◆ ◆

The man who does not read good books
has no advantage over the man who
can't read them. – Mark Twain

"Dear ParentLine," read a letter printed in the *New Hampshire Union Leader* (September 10, 2004). "My 14-year-old daughter has the toughest time doing homework . . . She doesn't even give the subject matter a chance. She just looks at the first page of a book and says, 'I can't get this stuff, it's stupid.' Then she locks herself in her room, sulks and watches TV. . . ."

ParentLine's answer was right on the mark, especially with this command: "Take the TV out of Tootsie's bedroom. Period. ParentLine's weary beyond words of discussing the negative effects of too much TV, whether the thing's in the living or family room, never mind the kitchen, bathroom and bedroom too."

"Street-smart"

Although some persons may equate "street-smart" with gangster types or with those who grew up in poverty, that is not how it's used in this chapter. Here, it describes anyone who lacks a formal education and yet is or becomes savvy in the ways of the world. With this in mind, contrast Tootsie's attitude with another 14-year-old girl to whom this book is dedicated.

The story of Isabelita Coello

Isabelita was the daughter of a widowed friend of ours in the Canary Islands back in the early 1960s. Isabelita was a slow learner, hated school, and was about to fail in what would be the equivalent of her freshman year in high school. At the time, I was using a few local girls who posed for pictures that appeared in Germany's prestigious *Photo-Tek* magazine, *U. S. Camera Magazine*, American photography annuals, and international photo contests. Isabelita wanted to drop out of school and work with me as an apprentice photographer. Her eventual goal would be to work behind the camera herself.

I didn't think she had much talent in that direction, but despite what some would consider a handicap—she was only 4' 7" tall—she had a bubbly personality, got along well with older persons, and was unusually photogenic. I had a long talk with her mother, who—considering the present situation to be intolerable—agreed that her daughter could indeed quit school and give photography a serious try.

The difference between Tootsie and Isabelita was this: Tootsie just wanted to drop out of life, whereas Isabelita merely wanted to drop out of the public educational system. She desperately wanted to become a photographer and was willing to do whatever it took. Although her abilities were limited, I let her work as a helper in the darkroom and as an assistant when I was shooting on location at an isolated beach. Later, when I expanded into wedding photography, Isabelita helped carry equipment and held the remote slave units for multiple flashes. Seven years later, when we moved to another island, I still wasn't letting the girl use the cameras because I didn't think she had ever grasped the fundamentals. Undeterred, Isabelita then found a job in the darkroom of a local photo processing company and struggled to learn all the ins and outs. Over the years, as we moved from one island to another and then eventually back to the United States, we lost track of our little friend.

Three years ago, my wife and I took a sentimental journey back to Tenerife, the island on which we'd lived from 1959 to 1971. There were a number of surprises. The first was that our long-ago friend Meli Rodriguez, who at that time was an illiterate and humble carpenter, had learned to read and write on his own and now—despite never spending a day in school—was the prosperous owner of a huge furniture store. Another surprise was that some of the photo murals that I'd made and sold 35 years ago were still in place, decorating bars, hotels, and doctors' offices. But the biggest surprise of all was Isabelita.

Although still only 4' 7", she was now the leading top-of-the-line wedding photographer in the entire province of Santa Cruz de Tenerife, even flying from time to time to mainland Spain to honor special requests. For Isabelita Coello, dropping out of school at age 14 was one of the best decisions she and her mother ever made.

Yes, hers was an admittedly extreme case. Here's another extreme case, one that veered off in a totally different direction.

The story of Tania Aebi

Tania Aebi was an 18-year-old high school dropout, a bicycle messenger in New York City by day and a Lower East Side barfly by night. She was going nowhere in life until her father gave her a challenge. She could choose either a college education or a 26-foot sloop, but if she chose the sloop, she would have to sail it around the world—alone!

You can read the account of how she managed to sail around the world in two and a half years with only a cat as her companion in her book *Maiden Voyage* (Simon and Schuster, 1989). Said a reviewer with the *Boston Globe,* "Like most first-class yarns of passage-making heroics, Aebi's story is a much deeper adventure of self-discovery that one finds only when pushing toward one's limit." *Maiden Voyage* was published in seven countries, spent three weeks on *The London Times* bestseller list, and was selected in 1998 as a Best Book for Young Adults by the American Library Association.

After such an epic voyage, did Tania ever go back to school? I wrote to her for an update, and this was her response:

High school dropout Tania Aebi, 18, in her 26-foot sloop *Varuna* as she sets out to circumnavigate the globe alone.

In 1999, I finished an undergraduate degree in liberal studies. I earned one year's worth of credit from life experience by writing a long, reflective process paper about the circumnavigation, writing the book, lecturing, navigation, getting a captain's license, and anything else I did that I thought might earn me the credit. I received another six months of credit through the CLEP tests in French and reading comprehension. In the end, I got the degree in two and a half years instead of four. Currently, I'm enrolled in an MFA program for creative writing.

I don't think school is useless. I do believe, however, that one needs to be ready to make the most of it. I was nowhere near being ready for school at the time of *Maiden Voyage,* but later, as an older

> and more-experienced-in-life adult, I really enjoyed the focusing of thought and ideas I got through structured learning. Both programs did not take place in traditional classroom settings. Instead, they were self-directed, where I planned a semester study at the outset, did the work at home, and met deadlines through epistolary contact with advisors and lots of writing. The law didn't require my education, but my mind did. It has been good for me to corral everything I've learned, to make sense of it, with the discipline of deadlines and feedback. So, I would say a formal education has its time and place, which is a different story for everyone. Educational ideas are of great interest to me now that I have my own children embarking on their own lives, and I'm also a great advocate of the simple life, or as simple as one can make it in this culture.

As Tania says, certain forms of education may be useful, but—as in her case—the young person may be "nowhere near being ready." In other cases, once you leave school, you need never return because you've charted your course toward an alternate port.

Public education

Author John Taylor Gatto, in the 10th edition of his remarkable book *Dumbing Us Down*, says that when compulsory schooling was first proposed in 1850, it was resisted—

sometimes with guns—by an estimated 80 percent of the population. Not until 1880 did parents surrender, seeing the militia take charge and march the children off to school under guard. "Schools," he declares, "are intended to produce human beings whose behavior can be predicted and controlled. . . . Well-schooled people are irrelevant. They can sell films and razor blades, push paper and talk on telephones, or sit mindlessly before a flickering computer terminal, but as human beings they are useless. Useless to others and useless to themselves."

The words of a madman? Don't judge Gatto (a respected teacher, by the way!) before you read the book. It opens with four solid pages of recommendations from authorities in the field.

When a formal education is required

Bill Gates, Steve Jobs, Michael Dell, Andie MacDowell, Tom Hanks, Sharon Stone, Jim Clark. Each either dropped out of college or was kicked out.

Jack London, Jimmy Dean, Richard Branson, W. Clement Stone, Sophia Loren, Sydney Portier, Julie Andrews, Lucille Ball, Humphrey Bogart. Not a single high school graduate in this group.

Nevertheless, if you plan to be employed by others, then a formal education is virtually mandatory. In addition—self-employed or not—if your goal is to become a professional such as a lawyer, a doctor, or a teacher, you have no other remedy than to press on. The law requires it.

If, however, you are a parent, and your children are not committed to a career in medicine, law, or teaching, consider the possibility of not only saving tens of thousands of dollars but doing your sons and daughters a tremendous favor as well. No joy comes from inept teachers, temptations to cheat, bullies, pressure from peers, intense competition, or being forced to study subjects that have no relation to life in the real world. *Of course* your children should get an education. It's just that a public school may not be the place to get it.

(Note to would-be lawyers: I have yet to meet a lawyer who's content and happy in his profession. Many would get out of the racket tomorrow if it were not for the money. A Nevada partner in a big law firm once told me that he had no friends at the office because "I can't stand lawyers!")

Education in another land

At the time of our 1959 move, the Spanish provinces of Santa Cruz de Tenerife and Las Palmas de Gran Canaria were great places to raise children. There were virtually no drugs in all of Spain, there was very little crime, and girls were not allowed (by custom) to date without a chaperon. We put the kids in a private German school, run by professors from Berlin known for discipline. When school let out, my wife held a class at home for reading and writing the English language. The girls were taught to cook and sew, and our son learned basic carpentry. All three took typing and piano lessons and studied the same book as Abraham Lincoln, who said about this basic text: "I believe the Bible is the best gift God has ever given to man."

Think about it: The children spoke German in school, Spanish in the streets, and were required to switch to English the moment they came home. We encouraged the children to read books on many subjects, and we made this possible by never having a television set in our home. We took trips to other islands, to the Spanish mainland, and eventually to both Europe and America. Although we took the kids out of school in their early teens, they have a more rounded education than some we've met who are university graduates.

The three Rs: Reading, reading, and reading

> When I get a little money, I buy books and if any is left, I buy food and clothes.
>
> – Erasmus

You are already a reader, or you wouldn't be reading this book, but wouldn't you like to have *more* time to read magazines and books?

For the past 60-plus years, with few exceptions, I've read for two or three hours every day. My wife discovered that fact long ago. We had just been married the previous day (simple ceremony, economical reception) during a November snowstorm and had spent an unusually memorable evening at the modest Flying Arrow Motel in Miles City, Montana. (I use the word "memorable" because we waited until after we were married to have sex—a decision highly recommended to all who are still single, divorced, or widowed). We trudged through the freshly fallen snow the next morning to a small café nearby, slid into a booth, and gave our order to the waitress. As soon as she left, I pulled the current *Reader's Digest* out of my back pocket and started to read.

"Umm, Jack . . . " said my wife with a wan smile, "what can *I* read?"

I tore the magazine in two and handed her the last half. That was her introduction to the fact that I was a voracious reader. I'd been reading since I was a kid. I read extra books all through high school, and I currently buy—and read—two or three books a week.

You, too, can find the time to read once you make up your mind to do so. In fact, if you study a specific subject for two hours a day, within a couple of years you can become an expert in that field!

One reason that I have time to read is that I do not follow any sports, seldom watch television, and almost never just sit around doing nothing. I read while waiting for my dentist, and even while in the chair during the times when she's not actually working on me. I read while waiting in line at the post office, and I read while walking in a nearby mall on rainy mornings. I read at every meal, during between-meal snacks, and except for the occasional evening of special activity, I read in bed for 45 minutes before turning out the light. But most of all, I spend a lot of time reading in the bathroom.

Here is the secret (and if you are a married man, your wife will like this one): I have my own bathroom, and *I always sit down*, even just to urinate. Since I don't have to watch where I'm aiming, I grab a book from the windowsill, pick up the red ballpoint pen in a holder alongside, and start reading and underlining. Perhaps 15 minutes go by, perhaps more. Doesn't matter. It's quiet in there. Quality study time.

Whenever I underline an especially pertinent point, I go back to the blank page just inside the cover, and make a note. Examples:

- P. 102 - *Ten time-wasters*
- P. 160 - *Hobby as a business*
- P. 224 - *Story of the janitor at a UK church*

Later, when I wish to review one of the many books I have on any certain subject, I go through each one, checking the number of notes I have on the inside front page. The one with the most notes is usually the best one on that subject.

Have you ever read a book from cover to cover, without a single unwanted interruption? I'm going to show you how to do that in the following chapter, but even now, you *can* create time to read. Unplug the TV. Turn off the computer. Simplify your life.

IF YOU HAVE TEENS STILL IN SCHOOL . . .

- Have a frank and open discussion with your children, using this chapter as a guide.
- Consider your options: Public school, private school, or schooling at home. Plan for the future. Will it be college, vocational school, an apprenticeship, a year's sabbatical, or might it be wiser to go straight into self-employment?
- After serious consideration over a period of several weeks, make a decision. Then implement it.

Suggested reading

The Teenage Liberation Handbook: How to Quit School and Get a Real Life and Education, second edition, by Grace Llewellyn (Lowry House, 1998).

You will not find this one in a school library because the first 75 pages are dedicated to explaining why school is a waste of time. (However, ignore the author completely when she endorses experimenting with drugs!)

10
THE NEED FOR SOLITUDE

◆ ◆ ◆

The great omission in American life is solitude . . .
that zone of time and space, free from the outside pressures,
which is the incinerator of the spirit. – *Anonymous*

Unless you've done hard time in the hole of a foreign prison or have sailed nonstop around the world alone, I have more experience with solitude than you do. At age 19, for one three-month period, I did not see another human. It was during that time that I made a decision that was to change my life, but before I get into that, let me warn you that serious meditation is hard work. The mind is like a balky mule—it takes a few licks and kicks to get it moving. And it takes solitude so that outside interferences will be cut to as near to nothing as possible.

"In so many ways we, as a people, have declared war on solitude and meditation," says Simeon Stylites in the December 1, 1954, *Christian Century*. "The worst possible calamity is to be alone. If you enjoy anything alone, you are 'antisocial' and ought to be rushed to the psychoanalyst's couch, or better still to the mental hospital."

Alan Valentine, in *The Age of Conformity,* writes: "Americans spend so much time in sodden absorption in radio, television and press that little is left for other communication or recreation. Inner resources for self-entertainment are atrophying from lack of use, and personal thought is being made unnecessary by the acceptance of predigested opinion from favorite commentators."

Young people today, following in the footsteps of their parents, often have the same aversion to solitude and meditation. Psychologist Robert Lindner says that one main source of youth's troubles today lies in "the abandonment of that solitude which was at once the trademark of adolescence and the source of its deepest despairs as of its dubious ecstasies. And frequently this solitude was creative. From it sometimes came the dreams, the hopes and the soaring aims that charged life henceforward with meaning and contributed to giving us our poets, artists, scientists. . . . For it is in solitude that the works of hand, heart and mind are always conceived. In the crowd, herd or gang, it is a mass mind that operates—a mind without subtlety, without compassion, uncivilized."

"We seem so frightened today of being alone," writes Anne Morrow Lindbergh in her book *Gift from the Sea,* "that we never let it happen. Even if family, friends, and movie should fail, there is still the radio or television to fill up the void. Women, who used to complain of loneliness, need never be alone any more. We can do our housework with soap-opera heroes at our side. *Even daydreaming was more creative than this*; it demanded something of oneself and it fed the inner life . . . [Italics added.]

"We must re-learn to be alone. . . . Certain springs are tapped only when we are alone. The artist knows he must be alone to create; the writer, to work out his thoughts; the musician, to compose; the saint, to pray."

Three months of solitude

I spent the summer of 1949 on a lookout tower on the tip of Williams Peak in Montana's Lolo National Forest. How did this come about? In my sophomore year in high school, during a movie that featured an awe-inspiring forest fire, I watched a forest ranger scoop up a beautiful young woman (Rita Hayworth?) and race ahead of the flames with her in his arms.

This, I said to myself, *is the life for me!*

Fast forward to June 1949. After completing three years at the University of Minnesota (St. Paul campus), we forest management majors were required to spend a summer working at an actual job in the U.S. Forest Service. During the three months I spent alone on a lookout tower, I thoroughly enjoyed the solitude. There was time to read, meditate, and even bang out an unpublishable novel on my portable typewriter. However, I slowly came to realize that a lifetime with the U.S. Forest Service was not for me. If only I hadn't gone to that movie about the ranger rescuing the damsel from the forest fire!

Thus, even though I already had credits ahead for starting my senior year, I never went back to the university. Many years later, I checked with some of my friends who had also majored in forest management and had graduated. *Not one* was still with the U.S. Forest Service!

The three-day plan for a business decision

I prefer to get away and be alone before making any serious decision, although not for three months. Three days are usually enough. Here is a typical trip, this one to decide on whether to continue with a present business or sell it and start something new. I take several books with me—some old, some new.

- *Day One*. I arrive at the Fairmont Waterfront Hotel in Vancouver, BC, early in the afternoon. I check into a corner room as high up as possible, take a 30-minute nap, and then head up Howe Street to browse in the indoor mall. In the evening, a quiet meal in the hotel is followed by a walk across the street to the Imax Theater in Canada Place. I am clearing my mind of any thoughts about business. Early to bed, read a novel by an author such as Grisham or Parker, and lights out by 11 P.M.
- *Day Two*. Up at my usual time of 5 A.M. I read and study one or more business or inspirational books before breakfast, during breakfast, all morning, and during lunch. After the usual nap, I head down to the shopping mall in the Fairmont's basement to buy a local magazine and read it over coffee. Afterward, back in the room, I watch the seaplanes take off and land for awhile, and then get out some paper and some colored pens. No decision yet, but I make notes about the pros and cons of selling this business, and pose some questions. In the evening, another feature at Imax, then early to bed, read a novel, and sleep.

- *Day Three*: Up at 5:00, read and meditate for two hours, then down for breakfast where I read my complementary copy of Canada's national newspaper, *The Globe and Mail*. Two refills on the coffee. Then up to my room where I put thoughts on paper, doodle, and draw mind-maps (connected circles) for the next hour or two. I come to a decision, pack up, check out, and head for home.

An alternative to seeing a psychiatrist

Sometimes, you just have to get away to preserve your sanity. Problems once got to me in my early years when I still worked for others, to the point where I was forgetting things and making mistakes at work. I told the boss that unless I took an immediate three days off, the mistakes were going to get worse. He agreed, so I packed my old car and headed straight for Glacier National Park. No tourists in early March! I arrived late in the day, set up my pup tent along the snowy shores of St. Mary's Lake, gathered driftwood, built a fire, and squatted down in front, staring into the flames. Three days later, I returned home and went back to work. Cured.

My wife had a lot to do in those early days in the Canary Islands. She kept our large apartment spotlessly clean, prepared all our meals, supervised the kids, held a two-hour English class with them every day, prepared for and attended meetings, and was my companion in our volunteer teaching work. About once a year, the pressure would start to get to her, and I'd tell her to pack up. Against her wishes, I'd take her across the island to a resort area, check her into a beachfront hotel, and leave her with a little spending money, her bikini, and some women's magazines and *Reader's Digests* to read. When I picked her up three days later, she was invariably cheerful, tanned, smiling, and eager to get back to work.

When did you last spend time alone?

One young woman in Los Angeles with three children lamented, "I've never been alone for a single day in my life." (Note to husbands: Ask your wife the above question. If her answer is similar to that of the L.A. homemaker, pack her suitcase, include some light reading material, and get her off to a resort hotel for three days. Tell her this is on orders from one J.J. Luna.) I would normally never recommend that you borrow money, but if there's no other way to do it, haul your TV sets and/or video games off to the pawn shop and try for least $200–$300. Even if you never get your things back (or *especially* if you never get them back), it will be one of the best investments you'll ever make.

Stopgap solution

One of my advance readers was a young woman who understood the need for solitude but hated camping (which might be unsafe as well) and couldn't afford a hotel. She said that "it helps to go away with a girlfriend who I haven't seen in a long time. While I don't get complete solitude, I do get some time completely alone and the three-day weekend is more affordable."

Another way—which I highly recommend—is to leave the radio off when you are driving alone. Pick a topic, and then meditate on it as you drive along. The best opportunity is when you are on a long trip. If I am alone, I bring along some CDs about business and self-help, play them for short periods, and then turn the CD player off and think about what I've just heard. If my wife is along and I need some time to think about a certain subject, I make sure she has something to read and I ask her to remain silent for a while. When I'm finished (which may be an hour later), I'll say, "Okay, honey, now we can visit."

If you have a van full of small children, however, give it up!

Camping, luxury class

As an occasional alternate to hotels and motels, I picked up an almost-new Scamp 13 last year. The Scamp is an egg-shaped fiberglass trailer that, despite its small size, has oak cabinets, a kitchen with stove and sink, a bed, a table, a propane furnace, 12-volt lighting, a toilet, and a shower with hot water. Since this little jelly bean is self-contained, I can park it in the forest, by a river, or along a cliff with an ocean view. It works out well whenever I need

The author's "getaway" trailer, hooked up in front of his mountain home in preparation for a trip to an isolated location along the Pacific coast.

to get some serious writing done, as long as I park it at least 40 miles from home. More distance is better because there is no substitute for putting space between you and your home territory.

Will solitude work for an extrovert?

To answer this question, I have had to go to others since I am introverted to the point where I avoid large gatherings and have never mastered the art of small talk. The consensus seems to be that total solitude may drive natural extroverts up the wall. Even here, however, *limited* solitude may be helpful.

It appears that some extroverts need to DO something for their brains to sort out information. Matt, a friend in Maryland, reports that his youngest daughter needs physical activity to process information. "We actually have her running through her martial arts kata," he says, "while she studies spelling. She uses each move of the kata as a letter, and the result is that she excels in spelling tests."

Another of his suggestions is to go to a hotel with a friend who can be constructive in helping you work out whatever your goal is. "Structure it as a working environment," he says, "say, three hours in the morning alone, then a break for lunch with the friend so they can reenergize with the contact, then three hours of solitude in the afternoon, etc. Extroverts love planning together, so they'll probably eat this up."

Are you one who* doesn't *wish to work alone?

Does the thought of spending many hours alone put your stomach in a knot? If you are one who thrives on interaction with others, you will need to be creative. Choose to work in a field where you have associations with others as you work from home.

One way to solve the problem is to start a business that calls for face-to-face selling, whether this means knocking on doors, calling on businesses, running a little espresso shack, or holding small parties in other people's homes.

Another way to balance the need for people and maintain your own business is to turn your home into a bed-and-breakfast. My first thought is that this would qualify for one of the ten worst home-based jobs in the western hemisphere, but to each his own—some people seem to thrive on it!

I once had a nephew who stayed with us for three weeks while he sorted out my mixed-up Excel and QuickBooks files. He was a party-type kid, used to having people around him all the time, and not about to change. Each morning, therefore, he loaded up some of my files on his laptop computer, grabbed a spare battery, and then headed out the door. When a question came up, he would call me on his cell phone from a table at McDonald's, Wendy's, Arby's, Starbucks, or even (heaven help us all) Chuck E. Cheese.

To each his own.

Conclusion

Although not for everyone, I do believe that solitude for the vast majority of you will help with frayed nerves, recharge your mental batteries, and help you arrive at conclusions based on logical thinking and common sense. This especially applies to the chapter that follows—the most important chapter in this book.

CHOOSE YOUR METHOD, THEN MAKE IT HAPPEN

- Spend an afternoon or an evening at the library.
- If you are the camping type, camp out of season or in a wilderness area.
- Go for a long drive. Choose the back roads, and play an inspirational tape or CD from time to time.
- Spend two nights in a hotel at least 40 miles from home. Farther is better. Bring along some interesting books. (If you've never read a book from cover to cover without interruptions, this will be your chance!)

Suggested reading

How to Stop Worrying and Start Living, by Dale Carnegie (Simon and Shuster, 1948). As an example of how to analyze worry, Carnegie says the first step is to get all the facts. Then, after carefully weighing the facts, make a decision. Once you've made the decision, get busy and carry it out, while dismissing all anxiety about the outcome. (Since this book has been sold by the millions, you should be able to pick up a copy in any used book store. Or go to www.Amazon.com where this new paperback lists for $7.99, and over 200 used paperbacks and hard covers start at $1.75. This book makes an ideal gift for anyone contemplating quitting a day job to go into business.)

11
CHOOSE A STAR TO STEER BY

◆ ◆ ◆

To accomplish anything, you need an interest, a motive, a center of your thought. You need a star to steer by, a cause, a creed, an idea, a passionate attachment. – *M. MacNeile Nixon*

Perhaps you are one of those people who are currently climbing a corporate ladder, hoping some day to reach the top. Imagine, however, your disappointment should you reach the top only to find that your ladder was placed against the wrong wall! Or, perhaps you have yet to choose a worthwhile goal at all. In either case, to be truly happy and content, you must find hope for the future and a purpose in your life.

That was the essence of the words from Marcus Aurelius Antoninus, who ruled the Roman Empire from 161–180 C.E.: "A man's true delight is to do the things he was made for." A similar quote is from John Masefield, Poet Laureate of Great Britain from 1930 until his death in 1967:

> I must go down to the sea again, to the lonely sea and the sky; and all I ask is a tall ship and a star to steer her by.

Before you start the home-based business of your dreams, I urge you to search for a star to steer by so that your business runs parallel to—or even meshes with—your dream. In a moment, I will show you exactly how to do that, but please bear with me for a quick review of U.S. history, along with a few facts about the all-time bestselling book.

"In God We Trust"

Unlike any other nation on Earth, the United States calls itself a Judeo-Christian nation. On April 22, 1864, President Abraham Lincoln signed the bill that permitted "In God We Trust" to be placed on coins, and a century later (1963), this motto finally appeared on all U.S. currency.

The final stanza of "The Star-Spangled Banner," written by Francis Scott Key in 1814 and adapted by an act of Congress in 1931 to be the national anthem, is "And this our motto be: 'In God is our trust.'" On July 30, 1956, President Dwight D. Eisenhower—in accordance with Francis Scott Key's words—signed a law declaring "In God We Trust" to be the official motto of the United States.

The men who founded America saw themselves as heirs to the Old Testament as well as to the New. (Thomas Jefferson even wanted the design of the seal of the United States to depict the Jews leaving pagan Egypt, just as the Americans had left the false values of Europe.) The laws of the United States are based on the moral laws stated in the Bible, and the vast majority of its religions purport to have a biblical foundation. Without that ancient book, there would be no Jewish or Christian religions or even Islam in its present form. (Mohammed declared that Adam, Noah, Abraham, Moses, and Jesus were all prophets sent by Allah, and that the revelations for The Holy Qur'Çn, or Koran, came straight from the angel Gabriel.) Here are a few of the many interesting facts about this ancient book.

The all-time best seller

According to the *Guinness Book of World Records*, the Bible is the best-selling book in the world, with more than 2,500,000,000 copies sold since 1815. It is also the book that is most often translated. In English alone, there are more than 500 translations in whole or in part, and the number worldwide is 2,355 and growing. Thus we see Rick Warren's *The Purpose-Driven Life* and Joel Osteen's *Your Best Life Now* on current best-seller lists, as well as the phenomenal success of the *Left Behind* novels. Although these and similar books may be just a passing fad, there is no denying the obvious: The Bible stands above and has changed more lives than any other book ever written.

Of interest to both you and me, it also claims to include history written in advance. In the 24th chapter of Matthew, Jesus spoke about a time when this present system of world governments would come to an end. The sign of the end's approach would be international wars, an increase in earth-quakes and famines, and a worldwide lack of love among one another. At the same time, Jesus' followers, hated by many, would nevertheless accomplish a worldwide work of spreading good news about a coming kingdom rule.

In harmony with Jesus' prophecy, the apostle Paul added additional details in his second letter to young Timothy. The quotes below are from a Protestant and then a Catholic translation of the original Greek.

> "This know also, that in the last days, perilous times shall come. For men shall be lovers of their own selves, covetous . . . disobedient to parents . . . despisers of those that are good . . . lovers of pleasures more than lovers of God; having a form of godliness, but denying the power thereof; from such turn away." (1 Tim. 3:1–5, *Authorized King James Version*)

> "But understand this: there will be terrifying times in the last days. People will be self-centered and lovers of money . . . disobedient to their parents . . . hating what is good . . . lovers of pleasure rather than lovers of God as they make a pretense of religion but deny its power. Reject them." (1 Tim. 3:1–5, *The New American Bible*)

I suspect that many of you have at least wondered if the end of this present world is indeed approaching, and if so, what your part might be in the larger scheme of things. Even if you dismiss the above prophecies as not applicable to our times, do not dismiss the power that its teaching has over myriad believers. Consider the following experience.

A fork in the road

Once upon a time, in a city far away, I found myself spending long and dreary hours driving a forklift truck at a sprawling compound known as Totem Wholesale Hardware and becoming more depressed every day. I began to question for the first time a vow made when I was 12: to always follow Bible principles no matter what the consequences. It wasn't the Bible I was having doubts about. My doubts centered around my decision to continue to use it as a guide. I knew—despite what the preacher in the First Congregational Church used to say, before I quit that church at age 11—that there was no fiery hell awaiting sinners. Rather, I learned that death would be just a dreamless sleep. That, I could live with. I felt an increasing urge to revel in all the pleasures the world had to offer: women, wine to excess, money, danger, excitement, and total freedom. And did I mention women? I figured that the money part would be the least of my worries because I'd already hatched a scheme to take out any bank in the state. I was so serious, in fact, that I sat down at the little table in my rented room, got out a sheet of paper and a pencil, and prepared to make two lists. On the left, I wrote *Keep on*. On the right, *Give up*. The right hand column was more interesting to me, so I started there.

No more working for wages. Gorgeous home on a Canadian lake. My own float plane tied up at the dock. Flying beautiful young women in to see me, a different one every week. I could smoke pipes and cigars, get drunk as a skunk, send gifts to my friends, have enemies beaten up, anything at all. I remembered a little ditty penned by Edna St. Vincent Millay:

My candle burns at both ends;
It will not last the night;
But ah! my foes and oh! my friends—
It gives a lovely light!

When the burning ends met at the center, I was not about to go to prison. I'd carry a gun at all times, prepared to use it on myself. Live fast. Die young.

It was past midnight before I'd finished the other column, the one on the left. If I stayed the course, instead of bringing shame to my parents, I could make them proud of me. I could marry, have children, work with others in a common cause, please my creator, have a clean conscience and a hope for the future: resurrection from the grave.

The difficulty in making this decision was so intense that it is still vivid in my mind today—the little room, the darkness outside, the scarred wooden table, the paper in front of me, the stub of a pencil with no eraser. Had I not decided, as did Moses, to forego "the pleasures of sin for a season" (Hebrews 10:25 *Authorized King James*), you would not be holding this book in your hand.

A note to doubters, atheists, and agnostics

Assume that everything I've built my life around is wrong: The Earth had no creator, Jesus was a myth, religion is the opium of the people, and we're all going to die and stay dead forever. Even then, here's what I've missed out on by what you may think has been a misspent life:

- No illegitimate children;
- No payments for child support;
- No sexually transmitted disease;
- No cancer of the lungs or throat;
- No shame to my parents and grandparents;
- No delirium tremens or cirrhosis of the liver;
- No gunshot wounds, no years in prison, no suicide.

An offbeat footnote: During our first year in Santa Cruz de Tenerife, I could see that the main branch of *El Banco de España* could be taken out in a certain way. I sat down one afternoon, wrote a short story about how that bank was robbed by a man using a certain uniform, props, and forged papers, and fired it off to *Man-to-Man* magazine in New York. Back came an envelope from editor Everett Meyers, and out dropped a check that paid our rent for the next two months. (I draw no moral from this anecdote.)

The secret revealed

If you decide to seek a star to guide you, the hardest part will be beginning the search with the conviction that you will follow where it leads. Earth-wide, the average for those who can do this is about one in 1,000, but if you are that one, then all you have to do is ask.

But don't ask *me*. Don't ask your family members either, or your friends, or seek the answer from any popular, secular book. Above all, never ask anyone who calls attention to himself with a title such as pastor, father, doctor, elder, reverend, or bishop. The only one to ask is the one who designed you in the first place: your creator. The qualifications for asking are that you be honest, hungry, and humble.

- *Honest:* You must truly believe that your creator exists.
- *Hungry*: You must be desperately searching for a true purpose in your life.
- *Humble*: You must be willing to accept help from any "common" person—even the old man who cuts your grass or the young woman who takes your money at Taco Bell.

Here's how it works: You pray directly to the creator of the heavens and Earth rather than to a virgin, a saint, or even to Jesus (who himself said he was only a mediator). By all means, send your request to the creator in the name of the Messiah if you consider yourself to be a Christian, but I've seen prayers answered by those who knew nothing about Jesus or the Bible. One such person was Carmen Reyes from Las Palmas de Gran Canaria.

"One day at the beach," she said, "I was watching huge waves rolling in from a faraway storm. I got to thinking about how some intelligent and powerful being had to have designed all this. I didn't know who to pray to or how to do it so I looked up into the sky and just said, "*¡Altissimo!* ['The one most high.'] Show me what to do with my life. *¡Amen!*" Two months later, a gray-haired woman stopped to chat with her in a parking lot. When Carmen asked her a question, the woman replied by opening a well-worn Bible and pointing to the answer. Impressed, Carmen continued to learn from her, and thus her prayer was eventually answered.

As for *your* heartfelt prayer, you'll know it's been answered when you can give a clear answer to the question, "What star do you steer by?"

ONCE YOU FIND YOUR TRUE PURPOSE IN LIFE

- You can then avoid any business that might conflict with your new objective.
- You may be able to combine your business with the goal you now seek.
- If you know in advance that you will need time free for volunteer work, you can do as I do: Plan beforehand to start a business that can be run part-time. If it grows beyond that, sell it. (Tip: Successful home-based one-person businesses are in high demand. They sell for up to hundreds of thousands of dollars!)

Suggested reading

The Bible, any translation that includes all the books from Genesis to Revelation (Apocalypse) and is not merely paraphrased. First read Matthew, then jump ahead to the Acts of the Apostles. After that, go back to the beginning, and read Genesis. (Keep in mind that each creative "day" was not how we mortals measure days, but was measured in millenniums.)

12
FALL DOWN SEVEN TIMES, GET UP EIGHT

◆ ◆ ◆

Most of the important things in the world have been accomplished by people who have kept on trying when there seemed to be no hope at all. – Dale Carnegie

When you saw the words "Work From Home at Any Age" and picked this book up, what did you expect to find? Were you at first disappointed to learn that I offer no magic "one-size-fits-all" formula? I hope that by now you appreciate that this small guidebook is actually about changing your entire philosophy of living—a map to lead you to that which can spell true success at any stage of your life.

At the beginning, when you read about various kinds of people who might benefit from this book, I assume you found yourself in one or more of the categories. Let's check the list again.

Still in high school

Unless you are committed to a field in teaching, medicine, or law, seriously consider not going on to college. (Even then, keep in mind that teachers are underpaid, lawyers are often miserable in their chosen field, and more and more doctors are quitting the field because of the endless paperwork and the exorbitant cost of malpractice insurance.) If your parents have set aside money for a formal education, discuss alternatives with them, such as allowing you to live in another land for a year, or going to trade school, or covering your living expenses while starting your own business.

Already in college

If you have second thoughts about the career you've chosen, or you fear that good jobs will not be available in your field when you graduate, read the advice above to high school students.

Single parent with young children

Never again drop your kids off at a day care center, and if they are in public school, plan, scheme, and dream ahead to when you can take them out. Work from home, school the kids yourself, and perhaps teach them to work with you in your home-based business. They will love it when you are always there for them, and they will learn the value of a dollar.

Parent of teenagers

Don't live your life vicariously through your children, or think that you are doing them a favor by helping pay their way through college. Why scrimp and save when other options are available? Why allow your children to accept student loans that will drive them tens of thousands of dollars into debt?

Unhappy employee

Don't quit your day job just yet. In fact, if you still have debts and are short on savings, slash your spending to the bone, and get a second job for nights or weekends. Knowing this work is temporary will lighten your burden because now you have hope. Work towards that happy day when you can tell your boss to take his job and shove it!

Handicapped

A cartoon in *The New Yorker* showed two dogs talking to each other. One was at the keyboard of a computer, saying, "On the Internet, no one knows you're a dog."

You can weigh 490 pounds and still run a Web site; you can be legally blind and still handle telephone calls; you can be deaf as a post and yet receive and send e-mails; you can be bedridden in your 80s and still write a book. Never in history have there been such opportunities for the handicapped as there are today.

Bored with life

If you can't help yourself, help others. Join a volunteer group, assist an older person, invite some neglected person out to lunch. As time goes by, you'll find that helping others will bring you unexpected rewards.

No star to guide you

Accept the challenge in the previous chapter. Ask, and ask, and ask again. Keep on knocking, and the door will open.

Baby boomers facing an uncertain future

Choose a field that excites your passion. Start out on a part-time basis. Read, study, and take action. The best is yet to come!

Retirees

You have at least two huge advantages over younger readers: a lifetime of experience and hours of free time every day. You may even be debt-free and have extra dollars in your pocket. Use those advantages, and, in view of your age, there's no time to lose. Start planning your future home-based business *now*.

Tired of living but afraid to die

At the beginning, I promised you that help was on the way. My prayer is that after reading this book and making plans, you will no longer be tired of living. If, however, you still are, then follow the foregoing advice given to "bored with life." There really is more happiness in giving than there is in receiving. Don't knock it if you've never tried it.

The one indispensable quality that you must have or acquire

In the first chapter, I wrote that there is one quality that is absolutely essential for success when working for yourself, and by now you will have come to realize what that quality is. Meli Rodriguez, the unschooled carpenter-turned-store owner has it. Isabelita Coello, the photographer, has it. Tania Aebi, the sailor/student, has it, and so did the American industrialist and philanthropist John D. Rockefeller (1839–1937). He said there was no other quality "so essential to success of any kind as the quality of *perseverance*," and added that persistence or perseverance "overcomes almost everything, even nature."

Another advocate and practitioner of this vital attribute for success was Scottish historian and essayist Thomas Carlyle (1795–1881), who wrote, "Perseverance and persistence in spite of all obstacles, discouragement, and impossibilities: It is this, that in all things distinguishes the strong soul from the weak."

If you don't yet have persistence, resolve to acquire it. When your desire to work from home becomes greater than the doubtful pleasures of your present life, you will want to leave your comfort zone and make the necessary sacrifices, so fuel that desire!

Starting up, of course, is one thing. Staying the course is quite another. I, therefore, suggest you print out the following quotation, and stick copies on your bathroom mirror, on the top of your television set, and on the dash of your car:

> Nothing in the world can take the place of persistence. Talent will not. Nothing is more common than unsuccessful men with talent. Genius will not. Unrewarded genius is almost a proverb. Education is not. The world is full of educated failures. Persistence and determination alone are omnipotent.
>
> – Calvin Coolidge

Nothing will work until you do. My sincere hope is that this book will call you to action. Must you give up wasting time and complaining about your lot in life? Absolutely. Dismiss the pain, and keep your eye on the gain: Work from home at something you enjoy, live simply with cash in your pocket and the satisfaction and contentment that come from creating and running the debt-free business of your dreams.

Ask, and it will be given to you; seek and you will find; knock and the door will be opened to you. (Matthew 7:7, *The New American Bible*)

Keep on knocking!

– Spring 2005

EXPERIENCES WANTED

If some of the suggestions in this book have been especially helpful to you, I would appreciate hearing about it. You may contact me at either my e-mail address or the Tenerife address listed on the following page. Please include your mailing address so that—if I use your experience in the next edition—I can mail you a free autographed copy of the book.

– JJL

For additional information about:

- Purchasing multiple books at a generous discount
- Using "ghost" addresses in Canada, Alaska, and the Canary Islands
- Ordering New Mexico limited liability companies
- Requesting special reports on Canadian bank accounts, nominee trusts, etc.

Go to:

www.jjluna.com

Or mail your inquiry to:

Tenerife Trust
P.O. Box 466
Burlington, WA 98233
USA

Contact information:

J.J. (Jack) Luna
(special editions; consulting; radio interviews; foreign and audio rights)
canaryman@swissinfo.org

R. Enriquez
(volume orders; ghost addresses; special reports)
canaryislands@hushmail.com

Robin Cheslock
(editing)
rijcheslock@comcast.net